Shine Youɪ
Touch Tl

Written and Edited By

Magnus Agugu

Pele,
Sending you lots of love
as always. You are a great
man that brightens up the
place with your energy.

Keep Shining
Brother!

Magnus
xx

Disclaimer

The patient stories I have told in this book have given me consent to use their clinical histories. To protect their privacy, I have changed names, transposed events, merged the stories of different people, and altered identifying characteristics. The techniques described in this book are no substitutes for professional care. As everyone is different, a physician must diagnose individual conditions and supervise all health problems. I urge you to seek the very best medical resources available to help you make an informed decision. Good luck on your healing journey.

Published by
Impression Publishing
www.impressionpublishing.net

First Edition published 2012
© Magnus Agugu 2012

Printed and bound in Great Britain by
printmyownbook.com

A catalogue record for this book
is available from The British Library
ISBN 978-1-908374-74-5

CONTENTS

ACKNOWLEDGEMENTS

"Stunned for words, an incredible experience, very remarkable. It is definitely a rarity when one can feel so liberated and at ease. J.

I wouldn't be alive if it were not for the combined love of God, The Creator, The Universe, Mother Earth and Father Sun. They have blessed me with these gifts and created this environment for me to play out my adventure.

There are many people that I would like to thank for supporting me on my journey as a healer. The first person I would like to acknowledge is my great grandmother Erebau. She is the ancestor that I channel and part of the power behind my remarkable healing energy. Many people who I treat say they see a warrior woman standing beside me. Sometimes they see other ancestors, but she is the person that I know is always present and never lets me down.

-To my father, Fred Agugu, for being a tremendous inspiration when fighting for justice and making your mark in the lives of all Ijaw people by helping in the creation of Bayelsa State in Nigeria. You have made history and your name is in the Bayelsa State Constitution. I love tenacity and unshakable belief in your dream to create a state for all Ijaw's to call home. Your legacy will live forever Daddy.

Thank you to my eldest sister Rebecca- you may be gone but you will never be forgotten. I feel your love whenever I see your kids. Thank you Felicia, for teaching me the art of re invention. You are a very powerful spirit who I hope will us your power to uplift our family. Thank you Michael, for looking out for me when Daddy left and for our good friendship today. We are so similar in so many ways, but yet so different. I'm looking for to many more good times with you bro. Thank you Faith, for having the courage to travel and settle in Australia. You have impressed me so much with how you have battled your demons and won. I love you so much and glad that you're on facebook too. Thank you for showing me that it was ok to love all colours, creeds, have gay friends and go anywhere without fear. Thank you Destiny for sharing your love for spirituality with me, when growing up. I miss you sis, but our time together will come again. To my half-sisters Thank Ebikobereie and Maria, thank you for looking out for me whenever I return to Nigeria.

To my niece, Genevieve for being like a little sister and coming down to Lewes, to learn that there is life outside London. Thank you Anthony, my nephew, for encouraging me to continue to be your colourful Uncle Magnus, no matter how old I get. Thank you Kingsley for taking care of me when I went to Nigeria to bury my father. I would have been lost without your love and light. Thank you Lloyd for looking after Mommy, when she needed your support.

A special Thank You goes out to my girlfriend Elle, for supporting me for over 3 years. You have been a rock in my life, by continuously believing in me to go forward and be my best. It was your power that got us Plantation Healing Retreat, our dream home. You too are a powerful spirit that has been sent to uplift, not only humans, but animals too. You have taught me so much for someone so young. Thanks babe. Xxx.

Thank to Gaby, for your friendship and support. I must also thank my ex-wife Cathy for supporting me right from day one, insisting I move to the countryside and appreciate nature. Thank you for teaching me how to market myself and helping to create the Magnus the Masseur brand. Many thanks to your family, for their love and support throughout our relationship.

Next, I would like to thank the photographer Steve Collins, for shooting my amazing book cover. It was taken on Devil's Dyke in Brighton and you knew exactly what was required to bring out the best in me. Everyone who sees that picture is impressed by the way it communicates the energy that flows through me. Thank you to Alex Tzavaras for painting me in the Bohemian Arts Studio for ten hours to create my back cover portrait. It captures my spirit beautifully. A big thank you goes to Ria Chantler for designing the book jacket, business cards and logo. They are stunning!

Thank you Tim and Debbie Snowdon, who were instrumental in creation of Plantation Healing Retreat, my home, and where so much healing magic takes place.

Though the images are not in this version, I would still like to thank the photographers and artists who have created such powerful images for the world to appreciate- Sarah Tate, Pete Griffiths, Paul Jackson and Andrew Deighton, Hugo Jones, Penelope Oakley, Julieanne Gilburt and Mark Golding.

Thanks to the journalists Lucia Blash, Nina Ludgate, Emma Smith, Rachel Branson, Angela Kennedy, Sam Underwood, Anna Murphy, Andrea Watson, Sascha Cooper, Alexandra Sawyer, Keleche Turner, Susie Oddball, Alex Strangwayes-Booth, Sarah Lee, Esther Austin, that wrote about my story, or interviewed me on their radio or TV shows.

Thank you to the event organizers that invited me to Shine my Light at their events; Claire Kirtland, Kyle Vialli, Mike Flannery, Kate Day, Mind, Body Spirit, Barcombe Feel Good Factor, Deja Hu, The Big Love Crew, Barefoot Doctor, and of course Zu Studios.

I would also like to thank the hundreds of people that wrote testimonials, as they are the back bone of my career and renewed my inspiration, at times when I wanted to quit and do something easier.

My life is a network of thousands of people, who have all contributed to me. During the 3 years it has taken to complete this book, these friends have stood out; Martin & Samira and the Zu Studios family, Ian Stephenson, Ray Phillips, Ben Conti, Mark Sequoia, Alex Ward, Earl Talbot, David Villa Clarke and the members of Creative Muscle, Ian Freeston, Jon Moore, Dan, Tom and Amal, Kim and Neil, Tigger and Mik, Dickon, Siggi, Wesley, Fadzai and Iamba, Jenny, Jason, Mark, Delroy, Imran, Jenny, Seer, Gesmay, Alaowei, Pele, Jeremy, Paradox, Kate, Tracy, my accommodating landlord and my neighbour Andrea.

-Peter Langdown for creating my website and Mike Freeman for clearing the viruses off my PC and keeping me online. Jorge Vallejo for drumming at my events. Black Wax for supplying me with an abundance of conscious reggae music to bless my soul. Chinwe Russell for assisting in making my delicious massage balm, Poitr for filming and editing my promo video.

Thank you Larry Lush and Peter Eyres for helping edit the final piece of the puzzle as I was really struggling and I couldn't have completed it without you.

But I would like to dedicate this book to my mother, Evelyn Ebideseghbofa Jonah Kalsor Agugu, for teaching me how to massage, telling me stories of my proud healing heritage, keeping the faith, constant spiritual empowerment and for being a powerhouse in my life. Thank you Mommy, for being the Golden Soul that you are. You are a shining example of how to live life and make a difference to all people who come into contact with you.

She spoke from her heart, with passion, whenever she told stories, as they were things that she had witnessed, first hand. Even today when I see and massage her, she will have a positive comment to make for me to improve my techniques, or share a story that has relevance, to increase my knowledge.

Words alone cannot describe the depth of Love that I have for my mother. She is a truly remarkable woman, who is loved by all because she loves all. I have learned this from her and my life has been extremely fruitful as a result.

Thank You Mommy. X x x.

INTRODUCTION

"What a fantastic experience! I came full of worries and woes and went away a different person, with a blank canvas to think through things. I am amazed and grateful and you play reggae too! I will be recommending you". S.B.

This book first and foremost is a celebration of my journey as a healer and the many people and lives that I have touched along my road. It is a first-hand account of my experiences with the thousands of people that have received healing from me, in its many forms. You will read about my life from the beginning and that night when I first found out I was a healer and the origins of my power. Few experiences have been so rewarding that I feel totally blessed to do what I do. It has been a privilege to be chosen for this mission and I fully accept the responsibility. Though there have been many challenges along the way I have remained focused on my journey as a healer and was sent here to do just that - heal, in turn, solutions have always been found.

I have chosen to give you the version edited by me, as this is how I speak. Having a stammer has shaped the way I speak and being dyslexic means that I have terrible syntax, a word I only discovered when a friend begun to proofread my book a few months ago. Although I achieved an O Level grade B in English Language, and haven't read many books, I warn you now that my standard of grammar may not be up to the standards you're used to. In fact the only book that I have read from cover to cover, in the last 2 years has been "Illusions – The Adventures of a Reluctant Messiah" by Richard Bach. Only then because it was a birthday gift and just 144 pages in length.

This book is an autobiographical account of my journey from before knowing I had healing abilities, to the moment I realized that I did and how my life has changed since owning my power. I do not profess to be best masseur in the world, just someone who has learned a thing or two about how the mind works and its effect on our wellbeing.

The intention of this book is to heal by raising your vibration while you hold it. If you hold it close and visualize yourself feeling well, this book may assist in raising your vibration enabling your recovery to begin. On my journey I have touched many and had the pleasure of helping thousands of people along the way. Many of you reading this will not believe the power you possess in your hands. I say, give it a try and focus your love for another through your hands and see what you discover.

My strap line phrase "One Massage, Many Possibilities" came to me a year after I began healing. Somehow the majority of the people I treated only required one treatment before feeling better. And on that first encounter new possibilities for their lives opened up, as they were set free.

The colourful pictures, my journey, the patient testimonials and magazine articles all communicate the same message; loving healing and empowering the human spirit. Most of the people I lay my hands on have a profound experience, some say it was a re birthing, others feel a connection with Source, others feel grounded and at peace. From these places all manner of healing is possible.

Healing is the ability to restore someone back to a balanced state. If you are someone that believes in science and respect a surgeon with multiple letters after his name and experience, then HE will be the best for you. Likewise if you prefer the services of a Faith healer then He will be right for you. If homeopathy is your thing you truly believe it will work for you, then it will and if you believe in changing your diet and eating organic and vital foods, then that will work for you. My treatments work because people believe that I can make a difference to them. And for some people my treatments work because they simply work, without belief.

Massage and hands on healing have been around since there have been animals on the planet. Animals lick wounds in much the same way we humans lay loving hands on a wound of a child.

We all love a hug as the warmth of another has a calming and reassuring effect that stimulates our own healing. This has always been known and practised. Life is a journey, so we are constantly being challenged, so illness is not something that is bad, but an indicator that something is out of balance. If we accept responsibility for our wellbeing, then we stand a good chance to healing ourselves, our communities, environments and world.

This is my understanding of how healing works. We are a bundle of energy vibrating, the higher the vibration the more vital we feel. When we're in a state of fear our vibration slows and we become prone to illness and dis-ease.

In the modern world that we live in with 24hour fear being pumped through our media, people can get addicted to the fear not realising that this is the reason why they are feeling bad. Even though they don't want to feel this way they cannot shift their mindset. But the moment they switch their thought patterns to the positive their vibration starts to increase and they begin to feel better. The sooner we start to raise our vibration, the better we feel.

As a conduit of Universal healing energy I see myself as someone who has been sent to give people a boost of uplifting energy, whether by smiling, fanning, dancing, massaging or simply listening intently to their needs.

Why are people so attracted to me? Well possibly because they see that I look healthy, radiate love and am usually happy. Being this way I am rarely ill, so walk my talk.

None of what I have written is fiction, though many may think I have exaggerated events but this is how my life is and the effect I have on the people around me.

CHAPTER 1
BEFORE I KNEW I WAS A HEALER

"I've been to all kinds of healers, chiropractors, osteopaths, and doctors for my pain. Today, I can sit without pain. It is something truly special. Thanks a lot". Marta

I was the youngest of six children from Nigerian parents who travelled to England in 1966. They were born in Rivers State and Izon, or Ijaw as it is more commonly known, and this was the language they spoke. Izon means Truth which is a trait that they were very proud of.

Their standard of living was much more comfortable back home as my father was a rising politician so they had a driver and maids to assist in the running of the household.

My father had a road "Fred Agugu Street" named after him in the Ajegunle Apapa district of Lagos, where he worked as a commissioner and he had great expectations for their future in the UK. They were good people that were well respected and loved back home but needed to travel to England to further my father's career.

They settled in a flat in Old Town Clapham but the first place that I remember was our flat in Brixton

They came with Rebecca, their eldest daughter and Michael, their eldest son but had left behind Felicia and Faith, with relatives. Destiny was born a year later in '67 and I in '68. Faith and Felicia were sent for over the next few years and the family was complete. Here in England things were much more difficult than at home and the change in culture didn't help my parents at all. My father came over to study and make connections with the Labour Party but once his funding ran out he found a job on the railway. My mother worked as an auxiliary nurse between bringing up the family and getting to grips with her new surroundings.

I was born on the tenth floor of St. Thomas' Hospital, opposite the houses of Parliament on the 12th October 1968. It was the same hospital that my mother worked at as a nurse and apparently I was so eager to get out that I was delivered in the corridor!

My parents had decided to have a maximum of six children but I wasn't the sixth child my mother gave birth to. Unfortunately for her she had two previous children that had died very young and two miscarriages, so was I very lucky to be alive. My father was very educated and was not going to give his second son just any old name.

I was named Magnus Woyingi Kuro Agugu.

I never knew any other Magnus' so couldn't understand why I was named that. I hated my name as a child, as I did not understand the meaning and when I was old enough to understand, I was daunted by it. Magnus in Latin means big, great and grand. Woyingi Kuro, originated from the Izon language of southern Nigeria, meant God's Power and Agugu, which roughly translates to "He who stands out and dominates" However, my understanding of the deeper meaning of my name is "The Great Power of God's Love", something that resonates with my heart.

When I came out of my mother's womb I was nearly eleven pounds in weight, but the labour lasted less than a hour, so thankfully my mother was not in too much pain for long. Many people I meet know that Magnus means big, so I am continuously asked whether my name was a fluke, as my parents could never had known that would have grown up to be such a tall man.

Back then the most enjoyable memories of my childhood was when my father and I were alone and he would buy me crisps and chocolate and take me with him to work. My mother worked days and father nights, so when I was young it was he that I bonded with.

He had a stillness and peace about him that I just warmed to. I loved my mother too but I saw her all the time so she was the one who would discipline me, so I felt much closer to him. I craved more moments like that but they were not forthcoming. My father was a known for helping others more than helping his own, a trait that I can see in myself.

When I was ten my father had done all he'd needed to do over here and went back to Nigeria. He was supposed to take us back with him, but chose to leave us behind and in the process started a new family in Nigeria. I remember the day he was leaving and I was crying in the kitchen. I remember asking my mother I did not understand the phrase,

"Going for good". I queried,

"Who's good?"

He was my hero and when he left a part of me died.

He'd write occasionally and even visited a couple of times. The first time he returned he brought over some giant land snails for us to eat. They were massive and in the morning had escaped from his bags and were all over the walls!

The second time he came over when my brother Michael was attacked and was in a coma for two weeks. My father was around for a few months on that occasion and the effect of having him around transformed my focus at school to such a degree that my grades shot up, and I was moved from the middle to the top band. It was the proudest period of being in secondary school as I was in the top four for most of exams. I needed the discipline of my father to really motivate me to try in school, but once Michael had come out of hospital he was soon gone and my grades slipped.

As a boy life was confusing at best, growing up as the youngest of six, in a very stressful household. Having a stammer made things ten times worse, as I had no way of authentically expressing myself. From my world, I was always a bad boy for breaking, fighting, burning or making too much noise. I was a big ball of energy desperately trying to find a way out of this prison. I remember on a couple of occasions being described as "the boy with the energy". Back then I had no understanding of what that meant, and the effect this energy would have on my life.

My mother would tell us stories about our great grandmother, Erebau, usually at times when I was standing on her back to massage away her pains. This was something I did quite regularly, though I had no idea that this kind of healing was something I would be connected to in later life. My mother suffered from various aches and pains because she worked so hard to provide for her family, so found great relief in the sustained pressure of my feet on her sore joints and muscles. Today I still massage my mother but at 18 stones, I no longer walk across her back.

My mother was a proud woman who knew she came from a rich culture and heritage, but was transported to this freezing little island with people who misunderstood her.

My mother's stories were a journey into a world that I knew nothing about, the place where my parents grew up and experienced life.
There, their beliefs were not the same as here and the old traditions are much stronger than growing up in London. People there worked the land and had a relationship with nature, the forests and the animals around.
One story my mother told me often was about an arrangement made with the crocodiles! This deal meant that no villagers would be eaten, if they left them alone! For years the villagers kept their side of the deal and no harm came to any of them,

even though they swam and fished in the same waters. This is part and parcel of village life in Nigeria.

In those days it was normal to seek natural healing remedies, so a wide knowledge of the curing abilities of plants was important knowledge that many people knew, which had been passed from generation to generation for thousands of years. Unfortunately as the dependence of modern medicine grew, much of the wisdom has been lost with the passing on of the elders.

My parents grew up in Rivers State in the time before oil was found and long before my father dissected it to create Bayelsa State. Back then most of the people were farmers and fishermen and benefited from the fertile soils which produced abundant crops. Oil was supposed to be the icing on the cake and the opportunity to develop the State but over the past 55 years all the village people have seen is their lands become the most polluted area in the world.

As long as I can remember, I knew that healing has been in my family for generations. My mother used to tell us stories of her Grandmother Erabau, who performed amazing healing miracles from her mud hut, at the edge of the Okolobri Village Rivers State, Nigeria.

Back then when I was a young boy being educated in London, though I found my mother's stories interesting, I couldn't help thinking that she must be exaggerating, because I never saw any programs on TV confirming this and my teachers at school had never mentioned anything like that in lessons.

You see in England in the 1970s the education system had never taught us anything positive about Africa. The slave trade is where the history of black people began and ended in the history lessons that I attended, even though there were great African dynasties that ruled Africa for thousands of years before slavery. Tarzan was how I knew about Africa and my view was that Africans were still in the dark ages, with backward technology and traditions. The people were poor, desperate, lived in mud huts, wore grass skirts, were uneducated and were savages. I cannot recall a single story or news item that celebrated African culture and medicine, so I wasn't about to believe all of my mother's stories.

I was a child of science, which we all believed was the only credible form of healing knowledge. I couldn't comprehend that African healing was something to be proud of. We were all ignorant in those days so the thought of going into school and even sharing that my Great Granny was a healer was just not going to happen.

In the films we were portrayed as cannibals, practicing voodoo or black magic and sticking pins into dolls remotely killing someone. As a Nigerian in school, life was just about getting by without being noticed. The other children would tease me for having an African surname and would laugh when my name was called out in assemblies. Back then I wished I'd had an English surname like the Jamaican's did. We Africans' had a hard time fitting in and school life was difficult.

Throughout my school years, I was a big friendly giant so was liked by most and even became a "Prefect" in secondary school. People were just not threatened by me and liked being in my company. I possessed an unusual ability to calm people but had no idea that I was giving off an energy that attracted all these people.
I was dyslexic, so although I could read, the words kept jumping around so I found schoolwork boring. Although not a fluent reader, I did like English and writing stories. I would sit there in class daydreaming about being somewhere else, living some other life, so used to love writing about it and couldn't see the point in so much of what I learned at school.

Having a stammer meant that expressing my feelings was very difficult, so I found that just saying yes to things meant that I kept people happy. I developed this outer persona to cope with

life, which was very different from the boy inside. Whenever I was confronted I would retreat into my mind and knew that I was safe here and only returned once the threat had gone.
Having a stutter meant that although I had difficulty in speaking aurally, I had no trouble speaking in my head, so would play out scenarios in my mind that never actually happened in real life.

There were a couple of other painful experiences that I remember when growing up. The first incident I remember was when I was at Ashburton Juniors School, aged around eight, and that day is etched in my memory and will never go away.
It is the day that the school doctor came and we all had ten minutes with him. I was trying my very best not to stammer by not saying very much, but he already knew and made a comment that rocked my world.
He said that had that it was a pity that my parents had not taken me to a speech therapist when I was younger because if they did then I wouldn't be stammering now.
I was filled with anger and concluded two things that day. The first was that my parents obviously didn't love me and the second was that my future was doomed.
I'd always lived in hope that I would grow out of it, but here I was stuck with this debilitating stammer for the rest of my life. To me that meant that I would never have a normal conversation and never get to be anything in life because all jobs required clear communication. Looking back my parents were stressed and just thought I would grow out of it, they said I had a cousin back in Nigeria who speaks the same way. I don't blame them anymore.

A couple of years later another incident had a similar effect that left me reeling.
My brother Michael was pretty much good at all things; sport, girls, he was an academic, loved by teachers and of course being the first-born son, adored by my parents.
We were in the front garden of our home in South Norwood in London, when we spotted this ugly kid with a beautiful girl on

his arm. My brother had remarked on this boy's ugliness before but today Michael was in shock as it was clear that they were in love. Michael turned to me and said,
"Magnus, it's not what you look like, but if you have the gift of the gab you can get any girl".
I didn't consider myself ugly but having a stammer, I certainly didn't have the gift of the gab, so concluded that I would never have a woman, ever!

Those two incidents shaped my future like a glacier shapes a mountain range and life became very painful, especially at a time when others were looking forward. I was never interested in girls and lacked confidence whenever I was around them. Girls liked me but I had way too many issues going on to let anyone get to know the real Magnus.

The most painful experience came on my 19th birthday when my friends were supposed to pick me up and go for a birthday drink. They were due at seven o'clock and I was very excited, so every car that drove past my house I thought was them but it wasn't. I was standing in earnest by the window and as the hours rolled by I became sadder and sadder. At that age I had very low self-esteem, as I couldn't afford trendy clothes or many of the material things my friends had. They all seemed to have a plan for their lives, but I was drifting with no ambitions for my future.

By eleven o'clock I was at the lowest point that I have ever reached and was standing in front of the mirror looking at my ugly face and tatty clothes then turned to my mother and said,
"If anyone in our family needs any organs, they can have mine!" as I was so sure that my life wasn't worth living and just wanted it to end.
My mother tried to reassure me that I was a great son with a beautiful heart but I couldn't hear her. I was convinced that I had nothing to live for and was certain I'd have a better life if I ended it now and asked God for another roll of the dice. I didn't

have the courage to commit suicide but considered how I could end the continual misery so prayed for a hole to appear and swallow me up.

I heard a quote recently that says "Not all flowers blossom at the same time." If you had told me that back then, I wouldn't have believed you, but I now know it to be true.

 When I left college I would go to the job centre every week to look for work and was rejected time and time again. So when I was offered a job as a porter, of a luxury apartment block in Belgravia, I clung to it for dear life.

The job involved security, cleaning duties and being helpful to the residents, something that didn't require fluent speaking. There was a switchboard but all I had to do was answer the phone and take messages, something even I could do though some people complained they couldn't understand me.

Finally, I had found something that I could do and possibly do well. The building consisted of twenty-five luxury apartments in the middle of the richest part of England. The residents were from all over the world and most were millionaires.

I was just seventeen so only had one plan, to do my very best and be the best porter I could. Within a matter of months I was part of the family and for some of the residents, the first black person they had known. I liked working there and loved the residents and soon the gratuities flowed.

Many of the residents were very wealthy but were very sad. They knew that having lots of money was not the answer to their problems. But whenever they saw me, they saw a man that was in love with people, which happened to be my job. I was working from 8am to 4pm but would spend some evenings there till midnight. Some residents saw the real Magnus and liked me for it, so did not perceive me as their servant. They would want me close and would take me to restaurants, let me drive their cars, use their apartments and some even flew me around the world!

I loved it there, as I was accepted and respected and my love for people was clear to see. Many of the residents who lived there certainly felt my healing presence. Whether they were a ninety-year-old English pensioner, Saudi Sheikh, Jewish CEO, Russian businessman, Philipino maid, chauffeur or builder, I treated everyone with respect and did everything in my power to help. If my primary motivation in life was to make money then I could have easily made millions of pounds with the connections I had made whilst working there.

But my primary motivation has always been to love people or find ways to help people.

There are so many ways to say thank you and most would give me hundreds of pounds in tips. Others would fly me around the world to show me how they lived.

When one of the residents flew me to Australia, I noticed that many people simply assumed that because I was big and black and not from there, that I MUST be famous, so they asked for my autograph wherever I went. I spent the first 2 days telling people that I was merely a porter and they were disappointed. So I thought 'what the heck' and for the next fortnight just smiled and said yes and signed my name.

People were just so happy to know they had met someone special. Being 6ft 7inches meant I could easily pass for a basketball player, so that's who I was for the duration of that holiday.

Another time, I was invited to Cape Town and had the good fortune of being flown in a helicopter around the cape, then we landed in the car park at Stellenbosch Vineyard. Chinese whispers got round that Shaquille O'Neill was in town and the head chef came out asking for my autograph. It was easier just to smile and sign and everyone in the restaurant was really happy. Back then I never laid a hand on anyone, but always seemed to have happy people in my presence. When you're smiling and feeling good it's much harder to be ill.

This was a very transformational period of my life, where I felt drawn away from the reality that had been presented to me from birth. Suddenly, I found myself questioning the status quo and looking to alternative points of views to how I could live my life.

I was around this time that I was introduced to Landmark Education; a personal development company that did cutting edge weekend workshops that had profound effects on those who participated. The organization was a breath of fresh air for me, a new beginning, and an opportunity to explore possibilities that were merely dreams before. Within a matter of months I was at the centre of a hub where I could learn, play and grow with likeminded and like souled people.

Suddenly the glitz and glamour of life with the millionaires seemed empty and no longer fulfilled me.

Dragging my body into work from Monday to Friday simply felt so wrong. Every morning was a struggle and I remember the routine of pressing snooze over and over till I simply had ten minutes to wash and dash for the train.

My spirit had seen enough and was telling me to leave, but I was too afraid, because staying there was so comfortable and I wasn't used to struggling for money.

I procrastinated for at least 3 years and because of this, it was my darkest period of working there. Before I was bright, smart helpful and really wanted to be there but I became corrupt, selfish, resentful and inconsiderate.

My body too was falling apart and an ankle injury I sustained in spring would not heal. Things got so bad that one day after a long shift I noticed a jet of blood squirting out from my ankle to the skirting board a foot away! I almost fainted when I saw it and thought I was dying! In total shock I went to Mayday Hospital.

I had a varicose vein in my right leg, which had collapsed. It wasn't life threatening but with standing all day on my feet, it meant that I would have to have an operation. This I took as a sign and after my surgical procedure I handed in my notice.

After fifteen years of rubbing shoulders with the rich residents of Belgravia, it was time to move on and the fall to my new reality was a harsh one. I was pampered and spoilt and used to easy living. The work that I did wasn't strenuous but very boring and I got too used it. I was a young man doing an old man's job. I had seen it all and it was time for a new challenge. The boy inside of me wanted to stay in the safety of the bubble that I had made for myself, but my spirit had other plans.

This was also the year that I got up close and personal with death as our family lost an amazing seven members over nine weeks.
We lost cousins, uncles and aunties and the youngest was a cousin, only nineteen, who jumped in front of a train because he thought there was no point to his life. I was at the same crossroad when I was nineteen, but thankfully decided to live on.

However, on April 4th, we lost our father, aged eighty-five, and my life sunk to even lower depths. Life was so miserable at that time that I lost the will to eat and look after myself so went from nineteen stones to just twelve stones. The fullness had deserted my body and I was a gaunt figure and some of my friends thought I had contracted AIDS.

Whenever someone dies in Nigeria, they put the burial on hold until their family return from overseas. As so many people had died in such a short period of time we simply didn't have the money to all fly over and arrange his funeral. So my father's body was put on ice for ten months until we could fly over and give him the burial he deserved. As a great man who eventually fulfilled his dream and dissected Rivers State and was pivotal in the creation of the newly formed Bayelsa State, his funeral was not going to be a tiny affair.

My life transformed again for the three weeks that we were out there. Over here I was just Magnus but over there I was the son of Fred Agugu. There were news teams at the airport when we arrived asking me if I would be following in his footsteps. The Agugu name meant so much more than I was used to back in England and I was overwhelmed with all that was expected of me.

The burial itself was an emotional day as you can imagine, plus I was over thirty years old and had achieved very little in my life and my father had done so much. Many of my family had five children by my age so I felt insecure about my life and not living up to their expectations of the British born son of the great Fred Agugu.
He died on the morning he was supposed to collect an award from the Governor, for his work creating Bayelsa State. There were dignitaries present who all shared stories about my father but I only wished I knew him a bit better and experienced the love he had for them.
One of the speakers was Goodluck Jonathan, the then deputy Governor of Bayelsa State and now President of Nigeria, and he stood next to me as we lowered the body into the ground.

In the summer of 2000, I left home and bought my flat. It was a time of new beginnings. I had been a living at home for far too long and had to find my way in life. I was a late starter, so chose to go for it in life, now I was free from my mothers' radar. Having been a law abiding responsible person, that always considered the feelings of others, it was not long before that I started experimenting with cannabis. Most of my friends started in their teens but I was a good boy so didn't start till my late twenties. Many people were shocked by the new Magnus, but were pleased to sit and share a spliff with me, finally, after all these years.

Dre, a shaman I met at Landmark Education, had left California and arrived in London for a couple of weeks, before travelling the world. He moved in with me for three months of that year and opened my eyes to other forms of healing and the challenging journey a healer has to walk. His lifestyle was his vocation and I admired him for having the courage to travel the world, sharing his knowledge and opening me up to spirituality. Dre was a tarot card reader who created beautiful mandalas, which illustrated what your year would be about. Many of my friends and family thought that I must have been insane to let this weird old man into my life. To them he was just a loser; a scrounger who was taking advantage of me because I was naïve, but having him around meant much more to me than they could appreciate.

We did a workshop together called Shadow workshops, which tapped into the shadow energy, allowing those to experience a re-birthing of inner power. The first six workshops were done in my flat until the classes became too big and we moved to larger venues across London and around the country. Though we had great success with the difference we made, it was not really how I wanted to express my healing to the world.

Life revealed more of my power when I became a nightclub bouncer (door supervisor). Although being huge and having 15 years experience in security, I wasn't a hard man.
I felt challenged when I become a bouncer for fear that I didn't have the bottle to mix it with men that loved violence. I was scared that I'd end up being exposed for being a softie when I was supposed to be a man.
But what I learned was that if you respected people then they'd behave, and it was the macho ego nonsense of the bouncers that created the vibration of dis-ease that lead to fights in the first place.
I also realised that I wasn't as afraid as I first thought and when required I could be every inch a man and hold my ground with anyone.

What really pleased me was on the nights that I didn't work, there were always fights but on the days that I did work there was significantly less trouble. It was clear that I had a pacifying effect on people, which was noticed by the owners, who subsequently fired the entire team, except me, twice in 2 years! I learned a lot about crowd behaviour and how I could affect the behaviour of large groups of people with my presence. Even with drink, drugs, loud music and all the distractions around I was doing healing and I had no idea that that was something I would be doing in the future.

However, the most significant memory of healing came in the summer of 2003, when my mother went into St. George's hospital in Tooting, South London. She was not feeling very well and walked into A&E complaining of severe headaches but within minutes of walking in, she was in a coma.
Later that day I received a call from my niece Genevieve saying that Granny was very ill and I should get there as soon as possible. I was engaged at that time, getting married the following year and the thought of Mommy not being present at my wedding had never crossed my mind. So hearing the doctors say that she had meningitis and that she would probably die this evening came as a real shock!

What I remember of that day was that I cried like a baby. Tears gushed out of my face like never before in my adult life. It was actually cathartic to express my love for my mother in that way. I remember standing by the entrance of the hospital pacing up and down in tears, dreading the worst and thinking how my life would be so different without Mommy.
I went up to her ward and walked nervously into her private room. What really surprised me was seeing my mother in this fever state, where she was like a zombie.
Yes she was alive but she could not recognize her family around the bed. The entire family was in a state of shock, especially as she is the matriarch of the family so to lose her would be a huge loss to us all.

We felt helpless, and could only comfort each other and pray for a miracle. No one was outwardly praying but we were all praying in our hearts for Mommy to make a miraculous recovery.

The next thing I remember was my cousin Mercy saying to me to stop crying and to be strong. As you can imagine the family were in shock, as we felt powerless after seeing Mommy in this way.

Mercy was the most senior family member present and was doing her best to be positive. She was on gown duty, making sure that my mother's dignity remained respectfully intact, and not exposing her breasts as she writhed around the bed in her feverish state. For some reason this really angered me and deep within I could hear my spirit shout, "Do something Magnus!", so instinctively I just hugged her and started to massage her, exactly the same way that I do today.

My strokes were in a circular motion, up and down her spine with my left hand on her heart. I had no idea what I was doing but it was something that flowed intuitively.

My fingers were tapping against her pressure points, meridians and chakras from her head down to the base of her spine and around her chest, solar plexus and her stomach. The massage only lasted a few minutes but it was enough to calm her and within half an hour she awoke from her fever. The doctors were draining some fluid from her spine and the curtains were drawn and I could hear her shouting

"Magnus, Magnus where am I?" in her loud commanding voice! Mommy was back!

She credited my healing hands for bringing her back from certain death, but I say it was her will to live that was the defining factor.

Either way, I was just happy to have her alive and well, especially at 67, women half her age were dying all around her that week in her ward. Even with this overwhelming evidence that I had healing hands, the thought of being a healer never crossed my mind and off I went to do my shift as a doorman.

CHAPTER 2
MY JOURNEY AS A HEALER

"A wonderful relaxing massage, amidst the chaos, competing bad music and crowd noise. May as well be in a closed room, with no sound of people for miles around. Excellent experience". Joe

Over a year had passed since my mother's near death experience in St Georges Hospital and I was none the wiser that my life was about to transform quite like the way it did.
I was engaged and living between London and the country making preparations for my new adventure.
We got married in the summer of 2004 and moved to a tiny village called Ticehurst in East Sussex.
We had a huge wedding, as we knew so many people. There were family and friends staying all over the village and a coach with 80 Ijaws that had come down from London. It was a festival and many said it was the best wedding they had ever attended.
My family and friends in London were concerned that I would get lynched as I was the only black man in the village marrying Cathy, a white woman , but their concerns were not my concerns. I came there to look for love and that's what I found as I fell in love with the people, the village and the lifestyle.

We rented the top floor flat of a mansion situated in the grounds of a forty-acre estate, which had a croquet lawn, outdoor swimming pool, herb garden and woods. From our bedroom window we had unspoiled views of The Weald. Living in the countryside was a major adjustment for me, as I was a townie that was used to the convenience of 24-hour shops, streetlights and public transport.

I had to re educate myself to survive there but it was a challenge I was up for. At night in a city it is sometimes quiet but the countryside is quiet on another level altogether.

The silence coupled with the darkness took some time to get used to, but once I acclimatised to my surroundings, I loved it so much.

Walking in the woods, hearing nature, breathing fresh country air and driving on winding country lanes were things that delighted my spirit and left me feeling at one with country living. Before long I was proud to say I was not from London and was so proud of myself for escaping the magnetic pull of the capital.

For money, I had just started a multi level marketing business that was earning me a thousand pounds a week, I worked really hard and did much more that was required so I could guarantee my success. Life was really looking good and I had my glorious future planned out. But within three months the dream was over and I was desperately searching for ways to earn money to provide for my family. Looking back I can see that God had a plan for me and it was not for me to be rich lording it on a country estate.

I remember going to Tunbridge Wells, the nearest town, thirty-minute drive away, walking into an agency to look for work. The recruitment consultant offered me two jobs; refuse collector or road sweeper, both for minimum wage. I was dizzy and in shock that just a few months before I was doing so well for myself and now here I was so low. I had to accept and signed the form and prayed that I would not have to clean my mother-in-law's street.

I went home exasperated and said to Cathy that I wanted to sleep in the spare room to talk to God, something I have never done before but I just had to find out why my life had turned out so badly.

I had a smoke out the window and lay on the bed and said
"God, why am I here? I'm the only black man in the village; I
can't drive a tractor, so I cannot be a farm labourer and have no
skills. There must be something you can do to switch my
situation from a negative to a positive?"
Then I fell asleep. About 2.30am I heard the voice of an old lady
saying
"Magnus, be a masseur!"
I awoke in shock, knowing that I did hear that but "masseur are
you kidding?"
I couldn't tell my wife that, we were just married and I'm sure
she would hit the roof. I kept repeating in my mind, are you
sure, as I may as well say I should be a porn star! I lay in there
for an hour hoping to hear another occupation that seemed
achievable then fell back to sleep.

The next morning Cathy asked,
"So what did God say?"
Bracing myself for a slap, I said;
"Masseur"
and she replied,
"I told you that you should use your hands on people five years
ago!"
She said that the first time I touched her that she felt an
incredible sensation and remarked that I should use it. But many
other women I had slept with said the same thing in the past but
I thought they were just humouring me, so never took it
seriously. I thought it was normal that couples said nice things
to each other whilst making love.

The next thing was to ring my mother and tell her about my
dream. She bellowed,
"Magnus you fool, that was your great grandmother Erebau, the
one with the special powers that I have been telling you about
all your life. It's about time you started your work!"

"Bloody hell!" I thought, my mother , Erabau and wife approve, so I sent texts to some friends in London saying I planned to follow my family tradition and become a masseur.
"Who wants one, while I train?"
I remember a friend sending a reply back saying
"Magnus are you up to your old tricks again?"
But this time I had a sense of purpose about me and was not going to be put off by other people's negative remarks and doubts.

I packed an IKEA bag filled with towels, some massage balm and headed for London on the train to see who I could massage; with no plan, other than to make it up as I go along. The first person had a bad knee and after 15 minutes of massaging the woman was amazed that her pain had gone, as was I.
In those days, a full body massage was done on the floor, on towels and I would do random strokes, though I found drum music very useful. Even back then I was known as the African Masseur and dressed in flowing robes and played a djembe drum CD, and to my surprise I was getting rave reviews by everyone.

It was an exciting time for me, as for the first time in my life I possessed a unique skill that set me apart from everyone else. Before that, I was known as a nice guy, with an open heart , but now I had these magic hands that were transporting people into other galaxies, healing their stresses and pains.

Before, I would be the guy at the party who would get everyone dancing, but now I had a more fulfilling and rewarding role as the masseur. I loved it, as there was queue of people waiting to experience my touch. It did wonders for my self-esteem and boosted my confidence around people.

I remember massaging a friend Mark Sequoia one weekend and him saying,
"Magnus, you're not a masseur, you're a healer!"

This I knew but did not want to acknowledge, as I knew I would have to make changes to my lifestyle, like becoming vegan and give up smoking and alcohol.

I really did not want to lose any of those things, as the thought of being one of those healers was so dull and boring. I opted for being an urban healer, which meant I could still live the life, without having to sell out to the lentil brigade.

My mother would tell me that the healers in Nigeria were pure and that my exposure to the western lifestyle had made me dirty, so if I wanted to be a healer like my great grandmother Erabau, I would have to spend a month in Nigeria de-toxing in the jungle. This really terrified me because the thought of giving up my western attachments seemed a step too far.

I have always been a larger than life character, who was both dyslexic and dyspraxic, although I only found this out when I was thirty-seven, so never really understood why I thought so differently from other "normal" people. I was blessed with a blank canvas, with gallons of colourful gloss to create whatever I wished and the energy to make it happen. I bought a really comfortable Darley massage couch and I was set and ready to rock and roll.

So here I was, this giant African man living in a country estate, considering his future. Starting from a place of anything's possible, I decided to use this opportunity and play big!

At that time I needed clients and, although I was popular, I had no credibility. No one knew me as a healer, so people were understandably wary of me. I didn't understand the processes involved and thought that because I had this gift, the phone would just ring with people wanting to experience a treatment with me.

Everyone that I touched said amazing things that blew me away, but I was on the first steps of a very tall ladder and gaining greater recognition would take a lot more than I anticipated.

As summer approached there were lots of fetes and fairs in the surrounding villages, so we bought a gazebo and a high stool and decided to market Magnus the Masseur that way.

I laid my healing hands on hundreds of people, many of whom had never met nor had ever been touched by a person looking remotely like me.

There was an instant fascination about me, as word soon spread that there was a credible healer working at whichever events I attended.

Many of the village fetes were set on the village greens with generations of locals celebrating together. There were stalls selling homemade cakes, clothing, artwork, raffles and a tug of war. On many occasions, I donated massages to raise money for their causes and entered the tug of war too!

They had never seen anyone like me before, beaming love and making everybody around smile. I have a deep connection with Kent and Sussex, since criss-crossing both counties to lay my hands on people who had requested my help.

Within months of starting my new vocation, I had my very first article in the local magazine. This was huge for me, as suddenly I was news worthy.

Word had spread to Tunbridge Wells, the biggest town in the vicinity and Lucia Blash, the editor of The Today Magazine rang me to come and do an interview.

The piece came out in the Christmas edition and it suddenly propelled me to a status that I had never ever dreamed of. Anyone reading it was left in no doubt of my potential and that the energy that emanated from my hands was something truly special. I gave Lucia a ten-minute taster massage treatment and she wrote a double page article. She mentioned "miracle" three times in the article, which really surprised me!

It wasn't clear at the time whether she had any issues when she came, but in her article wrote she could feel my healing energy working over two weeks later. She put her experience with me beautifully into words and I thank her for that because since then I have never looked back.

At a Cancer Charity event raising money for MacMillan Nurses, farmer, and former cancer patient, Lester Gosbee, converted a sheep pen into a Caribbean scene, complete with fake palm trees, limbo dancers and steel drummers and asked me to do my healing. There was a queue of about 50 people lined up to have a treatment, so they each had a quick five-minute taster.
To my surprise, the remarks and testimonials were unbelievable. One grateful recipient, Nina Ludgate, happened to run her own local magazine. Nina came for a proper treatment a few days later and wrote an article in her magazine.
She had an African husband who was finding it difficult settling into the rural environment so we had plenty in common. Since then we have remained great friends and have supported each other over the years.

Had I been a white masseur in the area I doubt if there would have been such publicity but because I was this 6ft 7 inch black man, living in an English village, people were very interested in my story.
I actually know a very good white male masseur, who is also very tall. He would massage using tuning forks. He had an amazing energy too and did great treatments as well but never received the publicity and attention that followed me.

Massaging soon became a way to meet people and soon I had friends all over Kent and Sussex. Many of the people that I touched back then are still in my life today.
Touching people and hugging suddenly became something I would do all the time as people all over wanted to experience my healing energy. I am always told that I give great hugs and although many men are afraid to be touchy feely, it was something that I have never felt ashamed to do. Being macho never worked for me so I learned years ago that there is nothing

wrong with owning my feminine and masculine energies and making friends.

  With the ability to make people feel great in an instant meant that I was able to unlock peoples' defences in a matter of seconds. Normally people wouldn't expect to have their stresses relieved so immediately, at a party or an event where they are dressed up. It's just not the done thing! The English are a very reserved breed. They just don't associate or expect to be at a networking event, where they are stressed out trying to impress and meet new clients, that they will meet someone giving African Rhythms Massage tasters sessions.

  It was a steep new learning curve I had to adjust to because I had to re learn who I was. My place in society had shifted and people really wanted to know who I was and where I came from and my beliefs. I was from the ghetto and hadn't had much time as this new Magnus. I was learning on the job and learning fast, but there are some things you only get with experience, so I knew there were many mistakes to make before I could fulfil my potential.

My presence as a tall African man living in the countryside gave many white people the opportunity to share their love for black people.
Many, I found, were fascinated about the African and Caribbean culture so were uplifted just to spend time talking with me about their experiences of encounters with people of colour throughout the world.
For some of them, all they knew about black people was what they had learned from reading the newspaper or on the television which was often negative, unless about sport, so to meet one doing something fascinating and interesting assisted in transforming their thinking about black people and themselves.

One of the best parts of being the only African healer in the area, was that I would travel to treat people who lived in

amazing houses all over the county. I was possibly the first black man that most of them had met in ages, so all those who had any connection with Africa suddenly wanted to invite me to their homes. On many occasions I would pinch myself and count myself very lucky to have the life that I was living.
A few months ago I was a nightclub bouncer being abused by drunks and here I am sipping champagne with wealthy, interesting and successful people. What a turnaround!

In the 35 years previous, I was known for being the big friendly giant, who sometimes stammered and stuttered and now I was known for my healing hands and for being a charismatic massage therapist living in the countryside, making a profound difference to the lives of people in my area. I attracted the attention of fundraisers and charity event organizers and was soon raising hundreds of pounds for worthy local causes.

It was no surprise that there were no well known massage therapist in Kent, but I was surprised to find that there were no well-known massage therapists in London either. In fact there were no well-known massage therapists in the entire country or the world to focus on! Blimey!

There is a Ghandi quote that says, "Be the change that you want to see in the world," so rather than complain about it, be that which you desire.
It was because of this that I decided to become the world's first Massage SupaStar. Someone who would be an ambassador for massage to inspire others to take up our discipline, raise the profile of massage, who was charismatic, confident and not afraid to celebrate massage in ways that have never been thought of before !
:-someone who would do charity work, raising money for dozens of good causes across the world, have lots of fun massaging, have their own style of massage, be featured in magazines, on the telly and may even have his own show.

:- someone that did fantastic treatments that would transform the lives of people they touched. But most of all is someone to inject some new blood into the industry, creating new opportunities for everyone!

CHAPTER 3
BEING A THERAPIST

"After just 15 minutes I felt like I was floating on a cloud. No pain anywhere". D.S.

There are different types of people that go into this industry and are blessed with different talents.

I am from the healer segment that has been blessed with healing abilities but, to be accepted and respected, needed an official qualification

There are many gifted healers who cannot pass the Anatomy and Physiology, required to be eligible for insurance. For them, the system can seem like a huge obstacle to fulfil their dreams to become a massage therapist or healing practitioner.

There are several other healing disciplines that, thankfully, do not discriminate if you have the talent. As a healer doing massage, I have found it extremely difficult shoe horning myself into a box I cannot fit into. We are all unique, so I have always been proud to be different and do my job as a healer, directed by my spirit.

It seemed strange to me, at the time, why people would see me doing healing, speak to the recipients who were in a state of bliss and then asked me am I qualified!

Surely the results are what count? I remember people asking if I was qualified and if I had insurance and me wondering if my great granny was qualified and had insurance.

In fact, I was very angry at the idea that, despite having healing hands that I had inherited from my ancestors, I still had to spend twelve months studying and pay twelve hundred pounds for the privilege!

I really found this a bitter pill to swallow, but friends were saying you'd better get qualified or you might end up getting sued and losing your home. Whoa! Scary thoughts! I tend not to buy into other people's fears, as my experience of people is usually pretty good. Though many of them meant well, I didn't let them project their fears onto me and continued on my path.

A voice inside of me said keep believing and looking for a way round this predicament. Surely I can find a way to work, whilst learning. I found an Indian head massage course, which lasted just a day for £95, an, on completion of that course, I was able to practise and get insurance. This was the break that I needed as whenever people asked those questions, I could simply say YES!
I continued to practice massaging at local fetes, fairs, pamper evenings and at parties and found that I loved my new direction. I was meeting new people virtually every day and getting to know many of the residents of Ticehurst and all the neighbouring villages. Many people were into Reike and tarot readings but I stood out because of my size, colour, African-ness and my healing hands, that were creating a reputation for them selves.

At one particular networking event I met Rachel Branson, who had just set up Wellbeing Magazine.
Rachel came over for a treatment and loved it and featured me in her magazine, in fact she loved what I did so much, that I had my very own column, "Magnus the Masseur says". Soon after this I had other magazines looking for stories and I was flying! Cathy was an artist and graphic designer, so knew lots about marketing and branding and Magnus the Masseur, was born.

We initially started as African Healing Remedies but whenever you mention Africa and healing in the same sentence people immediately think of voodoo.
So we chose masseur, as massage was not known for killing people.
t.

So Magnus the Masseur had a ring to it that we could both agree with. I knew then that the kind of massage that I did was much more than the basic Swedish massage and I would have lots of explaining to do as the difference between what I did and EVERY other style of massage that existed..

At first I treated friends and family, but as my face began to spring up in local papers and magazines more and more people wanted to experience my treatments.
Nearly all had very good things to say as when they would arrive in pain and leave ecstatic.

Robert, a retired civil servant had been suffering excruciating pain in his hands and wrists, and was due to have an operation for carpal tunnel syndrome. The treatment that he was due to undergo would involve them cutting the tendons in his wrist, allowing the hand to open fully.
This painful procedure would have his hand in plaster for six weeks. When I initially approached Robert, he was in so much pain that he didn't want me to touch him.
Later, I massaged his wrists for just five minutes and his pain went away and he could use his hand as normal. Six months later he wrote a testimonial saying that after six months his hand was fine with no more pain.

It really meant something to me that middle and upper middle class white people where writing testimonials about my treatments. Not because I thought they were better people than those in the ghetto, but if I was still living in South Norwood, people may have doubted what was written, but as we had no prior connection I knew they must have been real.
Doubters reading the testimonials initially think that I had forged the statements but once they experienced a treatment themselves they would soon realize that these were actually the thoughts and feelings of someone who had just been on a spiritual journey, not simply had a massage for their sore neck.

One of the problems that I ran into but could not overcome was that people came to me for 3 sessions but would only have the one, as they felt amazing, so did not need more.

An elderly couple I used to treat would joke that they would love me to come over more often but found that when I left they felt fighting fit again for such a long time.

I suppose that's the difference between being a massage therapist and a healer. I really needed their custom and genuine feedback but it seemed I was destined to be a miracle healer that people came to when they had nowhere else to turn.

This was very hard to deal with because I lost my confidence when telling people when to rebook. In many cases I wanted them to return the following week but found that they felt fixed, so they had no need to see me again.

My next obstacle was my understanding of the healing process. For most it was instant and for others much longer. Most of the people that I lay my hands on had a beautiful re-birthing experience. They would say that they had never felt better in years, but the following day some said they felt terrible. I found this hard to deal with as I tried my best to heal them but for some strange reason they felt awful. I knew that after a deep tissue massage that the muscles would ache the following day and that our bodies were just releasing the toxins.

I later found out that this is known as delayed onset muscle soreness (DOMS). This experience is fairly common in people who are not used to regular massages and is the same feeling that you get when you don't exercise for a long time. The pain usually subsides in 48 hours though some patients would conclude that this must have been due to having a bad massage when actually it was a good treatment with the muscles getting a good workout.

Since discovering this I would tell my clients to expect a painful reaction for a couple of days and to have a hot bath or visit a sauna to relieve their pain and to drink lots of water.

One client shared her experience with a respected healer who, after a treatment with , was unable to walk properly for 2 years! This gave me the perspective I required to understand that the healing process was not as straightforward as I first thought.

Healing is a journey back to wholeness, and adjustments in lifestyle were required to bring a person back to equilibrium.

I was never cut out to be one those therapists that do everything by the book, even though I tried for a bit but found that the book way was just not me.
It was not that I was doing anything wrong but I simply trusted my instincts, so whereas many people would have waited to get their Anatomy and Physiology before practising, I completed over one thousand treatments, created my very own style of massage, (African Rhythms Massage), wrote a column in Wellbeing magazine, featured in many other publications, all in addition to appearing on Sky TV and the BBC radio.
When I decided to do my Anatomy and Physiology qualification, I chose to do it over three months instead of a year or two.
Being dyslexic the thought of learning about the body in a scientific environment for twelve months would have killed me, so I opted for the shorter but intense experience.
Barvesh Joshi, who ran Body Basic School of Massage in Stratford, London, was instrumental in my journey. He possessed knowledge of the industry , coupled with a great wisdom of teaching to pass on what I required to try and follow my own path.

I remember him saying to me "Magnus, always believe you're the best" and that is a piece of advice that I have followed ever since working with him.

Paying a thousand pounds for the privilege to work in the Borough of Westminster in Central London was the price all top therapists had to pay.

But the annoying thing was that I already knew how to massage, and the Swedish style had too few strokes for me to do what I do best. It was a routine, which frankly I found rather dull. Many therapists I spoke to after they qualified said the same thing but unfortunately it's the same in many industries.

So there I was armed with my ITEC Massage Diploma enabling me to work in London and having full insurance.
Yay!
I was legal and no one could say otherwise. Finally after all this time, I could hold my head high and fulfil my plan to work for wealthy people who could pay me what I thought I deserved. But after a spell in Harley St I realized that money wasn't my main motivation and this direction simply wasn't for me.

There seemed a 40/60 split between the clients coming for physical ailments, and stresses caused by lifestyle.
Whist I did treat some sports people, as I was a healer/massage therapist, many people sought the services of a sports masseur or a deep tissue practitioner. For some people they expect to be left in agony after a good massage. Everyone has a different expectation as to what they regard as good massage. As a big strong man, I really don't need to prove how tough I am by hurting people, so communicate as much as possible to give my clients what they require without crippling them!

On one memorable occasion where I remember massaging over thirty people in one day, a man come to me at Bodium Village fete; I had set up my gazebo and was doing ten-minute treatments to promote myself.
Jack, a seventeen year old skate boarder, had recently broken his hand and had his wrist in plaster. He was experiencing constant pain, which painkillers could not help but in less than five minutes of stroking my hand over his injury his pain went!
I told Jack to visualize himself skate boarding again, fully fit and back to being the lad full of smiles again. It was one of

those moments that make being a healer so special. There was a reiki master there who came over for a taster and remarked;

"Magnus, you possess the true healing energy."

At charity fundraiser for Kent Handicapped Sharing Association in Chevening, over a thousand people showed up to support this good cause on this hot summer's Sunday.
The sun shone brightly, the queues gathered, and all had their stresses removed by my healing hands.
David, a cantankerous old man, heard something about a healer being present who may be able to do something to help his back.
He was an 84-year-old gentleman who was suffering immense lower back pain, which had been giving him problems for over twenty years.
He used to be a builder and so was used to hard physical work, so as he aged didn't give his body a rest, only to find his back eventually giving in.
When people are in excruciating pain all they want is to get rid of it and are willing to try anything.

David would not normally book the services of an African healer, but had been visiting a specialist in London who was giving him injections every few months.
This wasn't working, so he was open to try my massage.
I find people tend to be less prejudiced when they are in pain.
He arrived early so had to be the very first to have his massage and didn't mind waiting while we set up. There were crowds of English pensioners gathered who were also interested to find out what exactly this African healer could actually do, as they too had their various pains. I sat him on my stool and just told him look forward to his 85th birthday, with all his family, friends and grandchildren around, to see all the faces that mattered, the three tiered cake and him cutting it, and his family singing happy birthday to him.

Once his mind was focused on his bright future, I laid my right hand on his temple and the other on his lower back, spread my fingers and started to massage his back in a clockwise motion. Within thirty seconds he was smiling and within two minutes grinning profusely.

As I made contact there was a connection with the universe that was so strong that it had the power to achieve almost anything. Healing energy was transmitted and Erabau got to work and gave David exactly what healing his body required. I was merely the conduit for this exchange but the entire treatment only lasted about ten minutes but it seemed like David had just lost twenty years!

In my life I have witnessed many people in pain but what I find most satisfying is when you remove somebody's pain there and then. I know that David saw his 85th birthday because he saw it so clearly in his mind.

He could see each smiling face, whilst pain free, standing tall. This was the message that I had to deliver to him that day. He sprung off the stool and remarked, "You're Good", then skipped off as aching pensioners overwhelmed me.

I was so busy that afternoon removing pain from the many senior citizens that I never even had time to go inside and view the beautiful mansion. As the most enjoyable and rewarding part of my work is connecting with real people, I wasn't that bothered.

I have a saying; "where I find people, I find pain". So I am always prepared to touch someone who is in pain.

I have had the pleasure to heal in some interesting places and with some very interesting people.

Living in the country meant that I was one of a very small number of ethnic minorities, so what a treat it was for the old ladies of Goudhurst to have a African traveller in their little village hall.

Though it could put some people off, I saw it as an adventure to enrich my life. Many friends I know would never choose to spend the evening at the Goudhurst Women's Institute evening meeting. Goudhurst is one of the prettiest villages in Kent, complete with its village hall overlooking the pond. It's a place where many pensioners have settled to enjoy their retirement.

Having several clients who were pensioners and knowing what a taster treatment with me would do for them, I knew that spending an evening with them would be lots of fun.
Catherine lived with Derek in Goudhurst and we met after she read about me in the Today Magazine. They were tremendously active during their working lives and were not the kind of people that we going to let their age get in the way of enjoying their lives. Although both very active, that's not to say they were not in pain.

Catherine sought out my services and came over to Ticehurst for a treatment. She had spent some years in Nigeria, so was very interested in my journey.
The African drums that were playing throughout her treatment took her back fifty years to her time in Africa. The full body Africa Rhythms massage that I gave her intuitively sought out her aching joints and relaxed her mind.
Once the pain had gone I turned my attention to sending her healing energy. Catherine left that afternoon feeling lighter and ready for her next adventure, with the sounds of Africa ringing in her ears.
Catherine was the one who thought it would be good for me to do a talk and demo at the W.I. meeting and assured me that it would be a full house.

The Women's Institute was filled with very active members who still lead very courageous lives.
I was invited to do a talk about my healing journey and later give them some five-minute taster sessions. The women's ages ranged from fifty to over ninety years old and all suffered pain

and discomfort for a number of different reasons. Some had lost their partners and were still grieving.

Others were just stiff with arthritis and other chronic joint complaints but all had the same thing to say once they had their treatment. The entire hall was buzzing with women that had been somehow set free.

In Africa the elders are respected and their word is the rule. Over here we have the exact opposite stance. We are supposed to be civilized but treat our old like we're ashamed of them, dumping them in homes out of sight.

Respecting elders is something that has been ingrained in me since I was a child, so I have always enjoyed spending time with older people because they have endured so much and are still here to tell their tales.

Chronic Fatigue Syndrome or Myalgic Encephalomyelitis (M.E) was an illness that I had heard so much about and met many sufferers of.

They were driven people that had ambition but whose bodies just gave up on them. They were experiencing a loss of vitality and in constant pain despite taking drugs to ease that pain.

The doctors had no answers and they were constantly shuffling back and forth from hospital for tests from so called experts.

At a pamper event in Sussex, over a hundred people crammed into the school hall. Most were mothers who had children at the school and had returned to the hall for some quality pamper time.

There were beauty therapists there, make up artists, hairdressers, fashionable things to buy and various healers giving treatments. I massaged twenty-three people in three hours so each session was short. But in this short amount of time I still managed to clear Tammy's migraine that she had been suffering with for months.

She was so amazed that something she'd been suffering with day and night, week after week had gone after just a couple of minutes. She then booked a treatment to come and see me about her M.E. In just two hours I made the breakthrough she had waited years for. It seemed like I'd breathed life back in to her and she was making a miraculous recovery.

The healing journey sometimes involves many repeat visits and a sustained lifestyle change that many are not willing to do.

Language is sometimes a barrier to communication, but thankfully healing transcends this. I have treated several people who couldn't speak a word of English and I couldn't fully understand what they were saying to me.
One such man was Mehmet, who I met at a cultural gathering in Hastings. This Bring a Dish event was the only opportunity to meet with peoples of different nationalities and others facing similar challenges settling in to the English society.
There were many immigrants present where English was not their first language. Mehmet fought in the civil war back home in Ethiopia and was suffering from post-traumatic stress disorder. Many of his family were killed and he fled to England, as he too would have been killed if he stayed behind. He was suffering from constant headaches, nightmares and it was easy to see the fear in his eyes.
He was a shadow of the former Mehmet growing up back home. Here he was a broken man, fearful of adjusting to a system he did not understand.

I lay my hands on his head and prayed for him for a couple of minutes before starting to massage his body. His body was rigid and it took a while before he was ready to let go, but as soon as he did I could feel wave after wave of energy flowing through him.
He was after the spiritual assurance that he had missed from his wife and family. That feeling that you get when a parent cradles a tiny child and they know that they are safe. By the end of the treatment it was like someone had just injected Mehmet with a blast of love.

His face was free to smile and his body at ease.

Thank you can be understood in any language and I appreciated his gratitude. The Bring a Dish events brought me into contact with many who didn't have the funds to pay for a treatment with me but as I was amongst this very loving and supportive group, it was not a problem to me to give my healing without expecting payment.
Sometimes helping a person from a position of pain to a position of freedom and peace is all the reward I need. I am a believer in Karma and know I will get my reward further along the path of life.

For many of my clients, the modern lifestyle was simply too much to cope with. Many people were on anti depressants given to them by their doctors, but they knew that it was doing more harm than good.
They lived in detached houses and drove 4x4 cars to do the school run, had the finest clothes and their husbands were businessmen but something was just not right.
Though they had all the trappings of success, their minds were frazzled. Most were very nice people who obeyed the law and did all that was expected of them by society, but realized that the health system had let them down.
They became ill and immediately went to see their GP, only to be given a choice between the scalpel and the drug. Almost all the drugs had vicious side effects that were as bad, or worse in some cases, than their original conditions so their immune systems started to shut down.

It was only after months and years in some cases, did they start to look at alternative treatments.
The mainstream media do not always show complementary therapies in the light that they deserve. Often you hear about the scare stories that may occur 1% of the time versus the almost

certainty of picking up a side effect from using allopathic medicine.

The world of alternative remedies is also vast and confusing so some are put off by the myriad of different solutions to their problems.

Coming to visit an African healer was the last resort for some, who had tried and tested many different remedies for their illnesses, but I am pleased to say that many left me feeling significantly better than when they arrived.

CHAPTER 4
AFRICAN RHYTHMS MASSAGE

"Thank you for a truly amazing experience. You found tension and relieved it that I was unaware of. Your power and sheer MAGIC in your hands is beyond words. The drums are a perfect accompaniment". Angela V.

My qualification at the time was a day course in Indian head Massage and for the ITEC Massage Diploma we were to learn Swedish Holistic Massage.

I could have called myself any one of these but there were enough English people doing these and I wanted to call what I did something that resonated with my ancestry.

After all it was where my family was from. I was blessed with healing hands, but was confused about what to actually call myself.

Healing was a word that meant different things to different people and many people found the term *healer* weird. Being of African descent, I was afraid to be labelled a quack or a fraud and only after people's money, when in fact I was trying to help people.

Many people that experienced my healing energy would feel better almost immediately, but I needed to create a treatment that lasted for at least thirty minutes to make it worth something financially.

When I did my treatments, I would play African drumming or reggae and found the rhythm a vital part of the treatment. Once the music started, I was in a meditative state throughout the treatment and the healing energy would start to flow through my hands as I massaged to the beat of the music, using many intricate strokes that were not taught to me.

With perfect confidence, I would find the areas of tension and pain and wipe away all pain, leaving the patient in bliss.
When I massage I do it with passion, whether the recipient is male, female, gay or straight old or young, dog, cat or horse! Everybody or animal receives the same level of focus and loving attention.
My hands would also deliver a charge of energy that fill their bodies leaving them feeling re energized and full of life.

Whilst studying the origins of massage, I found out that Queen Isis was the first recorded practitioner who used massage as a form of healing, some six thousand years ago in Egypt.
I was so proud to see this, but then wondered why none of the two hundred recorded styles of bodywork included those from Africa.
Why is it that everybody knows about voodoo, but no one ever talks about positive healing that originated from Africa? For this reason I wanted to put the record straight and knew that by crediting Africa in the title of what I do, people will start to take an interest in some of the other medicine, treatments and wisdoms other African healers might have to offer.

Before starting, I would always do a consultation to find out why the patient had come for a treatment with me and ask what they thought was the cause of their problem. Most would think it was of a physical nature, but I always like to refer to some reference books that I have to dig a little deeper as to the origins of the condition.
One such book that has travelled with me for many years is "You Can Heal Your Life by Louise L. Hay. This amazing book looks at the background conversations that are at the root of conditions. It is clear and simple and has the "probable cause" and a "new thought pattern".
I have found this book invaluable at times, as sometimes some people need to see in print, before they are willing to accept it as a possible reason why they are ill or in pain.

My healing hands would usually sort out the problem but I always like to remind people that it is they that caused the illness and it is they that can cure it and not to rely on me to do it for them.

African Rhythms Massage is an enjoyable treatment to do as it is just like dancing. I found that doing treatments to rhythms not only stimulated my patients but me also, so I found it easy and I always wanted to do more. This happiness was communicated through my hands to the receiver.

For this reason healing doesn't occur as hard work but something quite fun. I sometimes do treatments without music but I find my mind wandering.

The energy that passes through me energizes me so there is a continual flow running through my body.

Many of the strokes that I did were in a circular motion using both hands together in unison or independently.

My fingers instinctively know where the chakras, meridians and pressure points are on a body and how much attention was required to give the patient the healing they needed. Having a seven-foot wingspan also helps when massaging the heads and toes at the same time.

If I tried to label every stroke that I do then it would be dozens, but there are a few common strokes that I use regularly.

Over the years, however, I have developed the confidence to massage people wherever I have found them.

Sometimes telling someone who is in pain to come and see me at my clinic I find is just not right, so I am happy to offer tasters at parties, festivals and even standing up on the middle of a dance floor.

Being blessed with a healing touch has enabled me to make a difference in a matter of seconds. Many find that booking a treatment with a stranger in a private clinic quite daunting, so to have someone willing to do treatments in a public place a refreshing change. I have never come across a healer that does as many treatments outside of their clinics. I can adapt my

African Rhythms Massage to almost any situation and pride myself for having the inclination and vision to do so.

There have been several books written and hundreds of scientific studies conducted about the healing benefits of sound, rhythms and drums.
For thousands of years indigenous cultures across the world used chanting, beat drums and danced in their healing rituals.
Today, in almost every town in the western world you will find people practising these very same traditions, to heal numerous ailments and conditions.
African Rhythms Massage combines all of these and I channel my Great grandmother Erabau's energy and, together, we heal.

The next logical step was to start to teach.
We set up the African Rhythms Massage Association and I began to write my syllabus. What I found so difficult was naming my strokes, as I intuitively massage so to stop and think of names for all the different strokes I did was simply impossible.
Teaching people how to massage is simple but teaching to massage like me is something completely different. Trying to earn more money by duplicating myself is something I know would be very difficult to achieve, so I put teaching on hold till I could figure out a way to share my knowledge and earn a living in a way that resonated with my spirit.

Fortunately for me I have found a way to teach African Rhythms Massage in a fun and exciting way that brings out the inner healer in us all.

CHAPTER 5
BACK TO AFRICA

"Magnus my first visit with you a month ago I had no expectation. I have osteoporosis in both knees, the right one being more painful. Happy to say that I have had no pain for 4 weeks and have taken no pain relief for my knee". E

Since becoming a healer I have become more and more Afro centric. Unlike in my youth, I was now more interested in wearing African clothing than western clothing, something which made me stand out even more. I only wish they made winter clothes too.

In 2007 I travelled to Bayelsa State, Nigeria to seek out and spend time with a native medicine man before starting work at The Hale Clinic in London.
My father's inheritance was being shared nearly five years after his death and it was a very important occasion.
There were several ceremonies involving all the senior elders of all neighbouring communities. All the oldest, wisest chiefs were assembled to hand over my father's powers to me.
My plan was to learn as much about the traditional ways of healing and to incorporate it with my treatments. But to my surprise, there was no one practicing native healing in the way that I hoped.

Just two hundred metres from my mother's home in Okolobri, they had built a brand new hospital.
People from all over Yenegoa, the state capital, would travel there for healing and there was very little sign of traditional healing.
Due the country's post colonial- Christian stance it was frowned upon to talk of traditional medicine and although elders did use herbs, allopathic medicine was what everyone relied upon.

For years this erosion of the traditional ways had been taking place and I was very sad not to make contact with anyone using the old ways of healing.

In the old days my people, the Izon tribe (Ijaw) were well known for their healing hands and massaging and many would travel to the cities to perform this role.

So it was very strange to me that none of my relatives was a practicing healer.

Most of my family was surprised to hear that healing is what I did for a living in England.

Given the opportunity to travel to England, none of them would even consider doing healing as an occupation but would have been happy to get a job as a traffic warden.

This I found difficult to accept, but for them, me being a healer was a wasted opportunity for someone fortunate enough to live in England.

I had many conversations with my cousins about our lost heritage, but that didn't seem to bother them as they were much more interested in laptops, mobile phones and name brand clothing.

My only saving grace was that in Wellbeing Magazine was a picture of me massaging Jeremy Clarkson from Top Gear and being auctioned for £3000.00. They knew who he was and that that was a very large amount of money for a massage, so I must be good at what I did!

In the end it was me who was massaging my family, who worked long hours in the fields planting cassava and tending to the crops. Many were in immense pain and could have easily massaged each other but none of them did. Instead they were taking painkillers for symptoms that could easily have been dealt with a twenty-minute rub.

Almost every day that I was there, I massaged someone and on some days I massaged many relatives.

They all were surprised that I could do what I did for them and I hope that, once I left, some of them would have learned a thing or two about hands on healing. My uncle was in quite a bit of pain and thoroughly welcomed his daily treatment from his nephew from overseas.

My father, Fred Agugu, was one of the founding fathers of Bayelsa State and a very important man when he was alive, so simply asking for the nearest medicine man was not as easy as it would have been if I was a tourist.

Medicine men are also known for doing voodoo and the Christian doctrine shunned any association with these people, although many seek out their knowledge when in need of traditional healing. This saddened me because I had come all that way for that purpose and left none the wiser.

However, my cousin Seigha said;

"Magnus, with the gift that you have, you will be massaging Kings and Queens".

Allopathic medicine has its place in the world but it has squeezed out traditional medicine to the point that many people thought I must be nuts to pursue this line of work.

Being born in England and calling myself an African healer, who had only spent a matter of months in Nigeria, it was important for me to connect with my ancestry, especially as I came from a noble line of healers.

My great grandmother was a legend and people would travel for miles to seek out her wisdom.

I had a romantic ideal that there would be others in my family that would be following in her footsteps but sadly this was not to be. If a tourist had been on my same quest, they would probably have succeeded, but because I was the son of Fred Agugu, there was no chance that my journey to find a spiritual healer was going to be successful.

After three weeks in Nigeria I returned knowing that I was the missing link to the traditional ways.

My mother's second child was a boy, who she named Woyingi-
Kuro (God's Power). He was a special child that possessed a
healing energy but he died when he was just two years old.
My family moved to England in 1966 and two years later they
had another boy, me, who they named Woyingi- Kuro.
My mother says that I was re incarnated and for years I was
unsure but now I know it must be true. If I stayed in Nigeria, I
wouldn't have been a healer but over here in England, I have the
freedom to be whatever I choose.

It is my choice to be a healer.

CHAPTER 6
MASSAGE SUPASTAR

"A massage which gives you possibilities is an amazing thing. I've never felt energy flowing through my body with such positively before". Z

"Massage SupaStar?? What ego nonsense is that all about?" is what most people think and that's not even how you spell *super*. At the time that I started massage there was no one around who was a focal point for me.
No role models in the public domain that were known for doing massage, resonated with me. Since then, I have come across several well known healers like Amma, Meagan Holub and John of God but back then, I'd never heard of them.

It was for this reason that I created my very own role model to focus my energies towards.
I wasn't always an alpha male and had to work at owning my new power. I took the best qualities of the leaders in life that I respected, the lifestyles they led and the difference they had made in their communities.
I then modelled Magnus the Masseur, The World's First Massage SupaStar on that. Maybe if I knew Amma I would have been happy to be Magnus the Masseur, or may have followed in her footsteps and have hugged a million people by now.

I have a happy spirit at the best of times and when I was plotting my path to being a successful masseur, I needed something to play for.
Simply healing twenty people a week and having a thriving practice, massaging dozens of middle aged clients seemed so

monotonous and boring and the prospect of breaking new ground excited me.

Very few people would have the balls to make such a statement, and I am sure I might react unkindly, if someone appeared from nowhere declaring themselves to be an expert at something I'd spent years mastering, but very few people think or act like me. I have a saying that describes me pretty well;

Magnus, you're too tall to hide, so you have no choice but to shine.

So once I started massaging, and quickly gained the reputation for being as good as I was, the rest all flowed neatly into place. People often ask me which agency is responsible for doing my Public Relations and are surprised to hear that I do it all myself.

For the first thirty-five years of being alive, I had never been in the newspaper before.
I lived in South Norwood, in South London, the area that I grew up and met most of my best friends.
Most of the headlines were about crime, murder and the usual scaremongering. I was just another brother living in a neighbourhood of other brothers trying to get by.
There were burned out cars just yards from my house and there were yellow murder boards up all around the area.
It was a pleasant area back in the day, but after years of no investment, South Norwood had become a ghetto.
There was no community anymore, but strangers living on top of each other.
It was a depressing place that I called home, but it never really felt like home. As soon as I left South Norwood and moved to the countryside, it was a very different story indeed.

Out there in Ticehurst, East Sussex, I was a successful black man living in a mansion in the country, had a unique gift to share with the world, was actually making a significant difference to people everywhere that I went and was enjoying my life.

For the first time in my life I was living a privileged life and my perspective had flipped. Gone were the concrete jungle and congestion, for green fields, woods, farm animals, country lanes and village life.

I discovered the English countryside and within weeks I was not missing South Norwood anymore, though I did miss my friends. I didn't have any more money, but my life felt so much richer.

As I was one of few non-white people in the surrounding villages, I was easily recognizable and soon I was at it again spreading my healing energy in the community.

Despite having a stammer, I managed to have an Internet radio show for four years. The station, GlobalGrooving.com was set up with my school friends from South Norwood.

My show was originally called The Bad & Beautiful Radio Show but when I moved to the country, I renamed it The Ticehurst Connection.

On my 2hr weekly show, I featured spiritually uplifting conscious music and an eclectic section, where I featured unknown artists. One lady, Carole, was an amateur singer who'd had a stroke a year before and was inspired to continue singing by her dying brother. Carol had a couple of treatments with me, which gave her the confidence to fulfil her dream.

She released an album and I regularly played her tracks on my show, which was listened to across the world.

I was beginning to make a name for myself, for giving musicians in the village and surrounding areas, a platform to get their music played to an international audience.

I have found that whenever I take on a project and I see it like a game and have fun with it, I can get my mojo into action and get it done with ease.

So the game to be the first massage supastar was a way to express myself.

Of course my ego loved this attention and does to this day, but back then it was difficult to tear myself away from that feeling of possessing magic hands.

Self belief is vitally important for success and if you're doing something never done before, then you have to be bold and prepared to accept criticism from all sides.

When it's you against the world then you must maintain a rock solid conviction that you can succeed, even though others may see you as crazy.

In many cases, I find that the more opposition I face the stronger my resolve strengthens. If I have an idea that I see no one else trying, I do not think I shouldn't be doing things this way, but exactly the opposite as I see it as something that no one has thought of yet, a type of creative marketing.

I now regard myself as a free man, as I have come up with so many different ways of expressing myself that are unique to Magnus the Masseur.

Charity was something that I knew about before, but just gave cash and I had participated in a few events before but suddenly here I was raising thousands of pounds for a dozen local, national and International charities.

When I met Penny at Benenden School for a sixth form pamper event, I had no idea what could happen from giving someone a ten-minute massage.

She had a very sore neck and had to drive for a couple of hours get home.

She was stressed but polite, so did not want to push in the queue of sixth formers, but I noticed her discomfort and moved her to the front.

Within minutes her pain was gone and she was smiling again and asked me if I would come to her place for a party. I came, massaged fifteen of her friends and she said she'd be in touch, as she had a way of helping me. Her husband loved massages too, so I ended up giving treatments to the whole family.

She was looking for interesting prizes for Helen & Douglas Children's Hospice Charity Auction and asked if I would donate a massage.

She said Jeremy Clarkson, the outspoken presenter of Top Gear, would be the auctioneer and said she'd try and arrange a massage for him, so he would bump the price up when the auction started.

Like many others Penny appreciated the value of being pain free. Sometimes I forget how precious feeling pain free can feel to something in agony.

She also knew that if Jeremy could experience a treatment beforehand, he too would appreciate the value that could be reached at auction. It was known that he suffered from back problems so would benefit from a massage with me.

Jeremy was too busy filming over the summer so the massage did not happen. It was then that I realized if I was going to be there at the event and raise a sizable amount of money, then I would have to up the game.

I changed my offer from a massage to a massage party, where I would travel to the winner's home and massage them and their guests. They were fully clothed massages, on my bar stool ,usually placed in the middle of the lounge. This was an even better prize so was put into the main auction with a reserve of £1000.00.

I am not aware of any other massage therapist that has offered such a prize for auction and especially after only being in their second year of the creation of the business.

The night came and Cathy and I set up in the foyer of the huge big top circus venue in Henley, situated on the banks of the River Thames.

I put on my favourite white traditional African suit which had been tailored by a Nigerian designer in Peckham a few months earlier. Being so tall and possessing an effervescent smile I am always visible but at an event where all the men are wearing tuxedos, I stood out even more than ever. It was a warm summer's evening and there were stilt walkers outside milling with the crowds and other performers present to entertain the people. The guests were made up of families associated with hospice, some who had lost children and others who had very ill and dying children, along with supporters of this most worthy cause. Though everyone was dressed up in dinner jackets and ball gowns it was clear that many were actually quite stressed and in need of comforting, so it was a brilliant idea to have me there to offer such a service.

At first people are always sceptical but as soon as the first person has a massage, then they all want one. Over the next ninety minutes a dozen people plucked up the courage to experience a massage, most of whom were friends of Penny, who were recommended to come and have their stresses erased.

Jeremy arrived with his two Top Gear co presenters, James May and Richard , but he was too busy learning his lines to have time for a massage beforehand.

I knew that if I could touch him then he would know what a massage with me would be worth, but he was fifty metres away from where I was and he was surrounded by fans wanting his attention.

He was trying to familiarize himself with his auctioneer duties and could see he was stressed as he tried to memorize his lines, so I wasn't going force myself upon him there and then, but knew I had to find a way to get to him, if I were to maximize this golden opportunity.

Once the guests had mingled and networked for an hour they were seated and dinner served.

The big top had a trapeze and acrobats overhead, followed by a couple of singers and comedian. The auction prizes were scattered around the room and there were some very valuable things up for grabs like paintings, artwork, and even a new Audi TT.

The auctions that I had attended in the past had prizes valued at no more than a couple of thousand pounds, but this auction was something truly special as some guests paid over £1000 to be there.

The founder of the charity, Sister Francis Dominica did a speech and played a video for us to see where the donations had been spent and the many families that had benefitted from the specialist care and attention.
Some of the families were people that I had massaged earlier on, so it was rewarding to know that I was on hand to give my brand of specialist care and attention, which was well received.

Finally, the moment had arrived for the auction.
Jeremy Clarkson got up to the podium and started the auction.
There were about a dozen items up for auction and I wasn't sure of the order.
At this point in the evening Cathy and I were at the back of the hall, out of sight, but I had a feeling inside that I should be nearer the front so people could at least see I was there and who they were bidding for.
It was my moment, so I decided to make my way across the floor past the thousand people to get to the stage.
The normal Magnus would have been happy to stand back and let it go the way it was planned, but the Massage SupaStar that I'd created had only one thought and that was to get on that stage and put my hands on Jeremy's shoulders.

JC announced "Lot 10, Magnus Agugu, the Harley Street Healer, who will come to your home and massage you and your guests.
Can I get £1000, £1100, £1200, £1300".
After a quick burst of bids the room went quiet and I knew that if I did nothing that would be it, so I instinctively walked onto the podium and started to massage his shoulders.
I knew it would have been a spectacle to see the 6ft 5inch JC being shadowed by a 6ft 7inch African healer. The crowds

laughed but Jeremy screamed!
"This is really good" and began shouting;
"Bid More! Bid More!"

The floor responded and a bidding war ensued between James
May and a businessman on table F.
It was one of those amazing moments you hear about when two
determined characters wanted the prize.
James ran out of steam at £2900 so it was the gentleman on
table F that won me for £3000.00!

That was the day when I truly became a Massage SupaStar!

I had a dream it and I fulfilled it. £3000.00 was raised in a
matter of minutes to help bring a little joy to the lives of many
families, who are going through possibly the most challenging
times of their lives.
I did that, and it was a moment to savour, possibly the first time
£3000.00 and massage could be mentioned in the same
sentence.
Before then people would wince at hearing even £100. It was at
this point that many of my doubters began to take me seriously
and realized that I wasn't totally crazy.

After the auction I continued massaging and was pleased to say
that my final treatment of the night was with James May who
came over to experience my healing.
He'd had a busy night, so his 15 minutes on my stall was just
the tonic to send him home to sleep. That was five years ago and
just last week I raised a further £2500.00 for them at this years
fundraiser.

This experience really gave me a way of getting publicity,
raising large amounts of money for worthy causes and
networking in circles where the clientele could afford my
treatments. I found it an easy way of getting great exposure, so I

found it a cost effective and ingenious way of marketing my brand.

Gemma had sciatica and came to see me at The Hale Clinic in London.
The Hale is the highest profile alternative therapy centre in the world. People would seek out many amazing variations in complementary treatments they had on offer there.
There were over a dozen massage therapists as the clinic had a reputation that was second to none. Gemma was a regular there trying out different treatments to aid her condition.

After she'd experienced her first treatment, she also saw the potential to raise money for her charity, The Round House Theatre in Camden.
Having been to a couple of events now I was beginning to be aware of what I could do to assist people to bid more for my prize.
I found that giving people taster treatments before the auction was the best way for people to value what they are bidding for.
Most are shy to start off with but once they realize that I can actually relieve their stress and pains in a matter of seconds, they quickly change their minds.
This too was a red carpet affair where each patron paid hundreds of pounds just to be there.
There were 3 tables of people that were interested in having my donation and it gave me great pleasure to go around playing them off against each other.

In the end I raised £3700.00 to offer underprivileged local youths ways of expressing their creativity.
Gemma looked great and walked tall that night. Her sciatica gone and in its place a broad smile knowing that she did a great thing that would benefit many people.
I was very proud of these achievements and the fact that no one else on the healing circuit was doing what I was doing to get publicity for their work and raising the bar for massage.

I am no longer known as the world's first massage supastar anymore but have revised the phrase to "Holistic Entertainer".

One annoying thing was that although there were people prepared to fork out over three grand for a massage party, neither of them actually experienced their prize.
They were happy to just support the charity financially and have a bit of fun for the evening.
That has been my experience at many auctions where the energy is high and people have had some alcohol inside them and want to bid on things they really have no need for.

I have had the fortune of being included in some interesting projects.
I have done some modelling for friends who are photographers for exhibitions and have been amazed by the quality of the photos taken.
Many artists too have drawn and painted pictures of me, though all very different, all have captured my essence.
As part of Black History Month last October I was invited to take part in a project called Positive Hair Day.
The project was set up to empower children of colour by celebrating our hair. Several members of the Brighton community took part by being photographed and telling their hair stories from childhood to the present day.
My dreadlocks have returned so was happy to have some creative shots of me with dreads again. These were compiled and made into two books and distributed to all the schools in Sussex.

Africa is always close to my heart so I have fundraised for various African charities, "Love is All we Need" a South African Aids orphanage was set up by a group of friends who were participants of Landmark Education.
I have their poster on my window as I am really proud of the difference they have made to thousands of children that have little or no support once stigmatized with AIDS and HIV.

At their fundraiser I arrived in my famed African attire and instantly started massaging people whist they sipped their champagne and at their tables.

As soon as the auctioneer announced my massage party, there was a buzz in the room as many who would have kept silent were bidding hard to win my prize.

I really love the opportunity to help those less fortunate than myself. I have also been invited to massage at a number of festivals and events all year round.

Sadly, in my line of work I have realized that not all charities have the interests of the victims as their main priority.

They may say they do but scratch beneath the surface and you'll be horrified to hear how much some directors are paid and the tiny percentage that goes to the cause you donated to.

To them it's merely a business and a way to gain kudos, whilst lining their pockets.

I created a massage promo video with snippets of me massaging at various events and laying my healing hands on some inspirational leaders in the field of health and wellbeing like Joseph McClendon III and Earl Talbot.

Becoming a holistic entertainer has opened many doors for me and connected me to many successful and dynamic people who would have passed me by.

Will Oprah Winfrey's make it onto my massage couch? Possibly, as I know that if she experiences a taster, she will surely want a full body African Rhythms Massage.

Whilst massaging at a David Wolfe event in London, I had the pleasure of healing the injured neck of Shazzie Love, England's top raw vegan nutritional expert.

She had an accident with her daughter on a helter-skelter about six weeks earlier and was still in a lot of pain.

I overheard her telling her story to friends who ran a whole foods stall and couldn't even give them a hug, as her neck was throbbing.

I immediately invited her over to my stool to have a massage before going into the auditorium and within ten minutes her neck felt fine.

It was the first time in a long while that Shazzie had felt this good and she soon was back to have a full treatment.

She came over with her camera and interviewed me after her treatment and put the video up on her VIP Lounge website.

More recently, I was chosen for BBC Sussex & Surrey's One Hundred Lives project where they followed a hundred people for a year.

As a recovering stammerer, they were interested in my challenge to do public speaking to large groups. During the summer, I did a 30 min demonstration and talk at the Mind Body Spirit Festival in London, so how I approached and prepared for it intrigued them.

The movie The Kings Speech came out and they wanted to have someone with a stammer on the radio show, but I would have appreciated it if they were more focussed on what I am working towards, rather than what holds me back.

Maybe this year they can focus on this book and my plan to sell millions of copies worldwide.

I finally watched the movie, on my own, but not until February 2012, a year after the hype had died down.

It was truly moving for me and difficult at times to watch, as I have had several moments where I have got stuck saying the simplest of things, like my name.

But I was left empowered in the end and glad the film was made to uplift others suffering with stammers.

I attended The Starfish Program, some years earlier, which was a 3 day residential course for stammerers.

I learnt on the course that there were two types of stammerer, Covert and Overt.

I was clearly a covert stammerer, as many people that knew me have never heard me stammer. The organisers were beautiful people and have helped thousands of people to communicate fluently and create opportunities for people that have suffered all their lives.

I have come to terms with my speech impediment and have learned to love it.

I know that it has done wonders for me, as it has taught me to appreciate other people's pain. Most people I meet don't expect a 6ft 7inch man of my stature to stammer and have difficulty saying his name, but I have found that it immediately shows my vulnerability, which in turn opens them up.

We all have vulnerable aspects of our lives, whether they are visible or not.

When looking back at this journey, I can clearly see that I have become somewhat addicted to the instant gratification one gets from doing the healing work that I do.

I love giving and as the endorphins gush out of my brain into my bloodstream, I get an adrenalin rush.

People respond so warmly having been healed that I want to do it over and over.

After many years of being ordinary and just trying to fit in, I finally began to appreciate my name and value the power vested in me.

Magnus Woyingi Kuro Agugu is a very powerful and beautiful name indeed!

I suppose there are many performers who have this same experience and their work makes an instant impact as to the way people feel around them. They experience the highs when they are in the zone, doing the things they love, but as soon as they're not in the zone, that glorious feeling soon wears off, so try and spend as much of their life playing.

One-day surfing facebook, I stumbled across Todd Brown and Massage Therapy Radio.

Until then I was unaware of how huge the industry was and that there were therapists that were being ambassadors.

They were talking about Meagan Holub, the world's first $100,000 massage therapist.

Immediately I contacted her and congratulated her on her achievements.

She said she'd heard of me months ago and thought I was the best Internet marketed massage therapist that she'd come across. Big praise from someone who has achieved what she has in the business!

I have always seen marketing of an extension of healing, as every time someone sees my pictures, receives a card or video of me, a little bit of healing energy is being transferred.

My logos resonate healing and friends have kept my flyers on their mantles to send healing into their homes.

Growing up in South Norwood, the only festival that I ever attended was the annual one at Brockwell Park near Brixton, South London.

It was a country fair with stalls, music and animals.

I was only ever interested in the sound systems that played reggae, but they were usually tense affairs with local gang members and their bull terriers trying to impress the girls.

So when I was asked to massage at the Wild heart Gathering in Sussex, I had no idea what country festivals were like.

This was nothing like Brockwell Park at all. It was small, intimate, friendly and there were families with children running around.

There wasn't a bull terrier in sight and it was set in the most gorgeous country estate you can imagine, with woods and a lake.

People were camped and everyone was friendly and smiling. I had never camped overnight before and planned to stay till late, then return the following day.

Kate ran the children's area and invited me to come down and massage.
When I arrived I noticed there was a healing area, so decided to enjoy the day but not massage, out of respect for the other healers who had paid for their pitch.
There were a number of people in our group and all wanted a massage from me while it was light and I felt very awkward, but stuck to my guns and only started massaging once it got dark, and the other healers had finished for the day.
I placed my stool next to a homemade pizza stall, because they had a fluorescent light, and offered my services for a donation.

It wasn't long before the first customer arrived and complained of aching shoulders and asked for a massage.
Once I'd finished giving him some healing, I was invited to work inside a huge yurt belonging to one of the organizers of the festival.
Spirit Horse was his name and in return for that kind gesture, I gave him and his wife treatments. I had no idea who they were, but they were so impressed by my healing hands, that they called all the healers from the healing field to come and experience a treatment with me.
I started massaging at ten thirty and by midnight I had finished, but had managed to touch some of the most influential healers at the festival.
Wildheart is the first festival of the season on May Bank Holiday, and it was the first ever festival that I camped at.
The festival bug bit me - there was no going back, so since then I have averaged about four festivals a year.

Many more people have experienced my healing, without me laying a hand on them.

Some have felt my presence in my being at parties, events, and festivals and out and about in the street, the high energy image on my cards, on Facebook, by receiving an uplifting text message from me, or by one to one conversation.

When I am around music, my powers seem to amplify and things get really interesting!

When I am walking around without music, I am rather heavy handed and clumsy but once I can hear music I become so much more graceful.

My spirit connects with music instantly and it feels as if I am tapping into a free source of energy.

I feel lighter and freer and able to channel healing to a large group of people with ease.

The beats found in tribal music summon up the warriors in my ancestry and together we give people the space to set themselves free.

Dancing is a wonderful way to give healing, as you can see the transformational journey from someone being shy and stiff, all the way up to really letting themselves go and flowing to the music, like an autumn leaf blowing in the wind.

People really want to let go and be set free, but often, they live in their heads, needing alcohol and drugs to connect with their souls.

Once I arrive, I begin my magic and get everyone included in the healing. Sometimes it can be as a smile as I look into your soul and for others I could take your hand and invite you up for a dance.

Once everybody is up and has let them selves go to the point of sweating, then I know it's time to bring out my fan and start taking the vibes to a higher level.

For many years I have attended parties and experienced some major shifts, depending on the energy of the atmosphere. My fan has been instrumental in enabling people to reach that little bit higher to a place they have never been before.

Within a year of moving to Brighton I met Marcus, a reggae lover with a huge heart.

Marcus had severe back problems due to sleeping on a futon and living in a flat with sloping ceilings. He used to have massages and would insist I use a great deal of pressure to ease the deeper tissues that others could not reach.

It was with Marcus that I perfected massaging with my forearms as Marcus had a high pain threshold and required more than just strong fingers.

Most people were more than happy with the strength from my hands so it was great to practice my no hands technique.

We met on the dance floor at a number of reggae events where I fanned and once we became friends, were interested in creating our very own space to people to dance.

Many of the women that we knew would complain about not being able to express themselves at clubs, as some guys would take things too far, when all they want is to dance.

They really loved to dance, but knew their writhing bodies could send some men crazy!

I have found that my presence on the dance-floor, as an alpha male who is smiling and sending out good vibrations, created a safety zone for all who want to just dance.

Together we created Pure Natural Vibes, our attempt at creating a space for people to really express themselves to conscious reggae, funk and kwaito music.

We did fifteen parties that were all wonderful to experience.

I enjoyed them as we succeeded in creating a place that people could come to and feel free to express their love for the music we played.

We had live drummers accompanying the djs and I would play the second set of spiritually uplifting reggae music.

Other promoters who had nights on in Brighton would also come along to support the One Love vibe.

The venues in Brighton were all licensed, so the selling of alcohol was their main priority.

I drink myself, but knew if I found the right location, they could be much, much better.

So after Marcus returned to South Africa I took time out to find that perfect venue.

I manifested my dream venue, Zu Studios, an art warehouse on the banks of the River Ouse which has the most sublime loving energy emanating from its walls.

The community Zu Studios attracts, are some of the most colourful and beautiful people that I have ever met and so have created the perfect venue for sharing the Pure Natural Vibes.

I cannot remember the very first time I started fanning, but it has been nearly ten years.

My mother brought back an assortment of colourful fans, when she returned from Nigeria one year and one of them resonated with me.

I found myself carrying it around my neck wherever I went and it soon became another tool for healing. By tapping into this free energy that exists inside music, I have found that I can dance and fan continuously for over 6 hours.

The energy flows through me and is driven by the beats in the music, not from my stored energy in my muscles.

With this blast of cool air, people are free to go further and reach higher.

Nights out with my fan are always memorable experiences, as many who have witnessed this healing phenomenon know me as The Fan Man, the person you will most want to meet on a dance floor.

When I was a bouncer I would patrol and make eye contact with everyone to make sure they were ok.

I do exactly the same thing with the fan, except with the fan I can heal more people at any one time.

My healing energy flows through my hands and is amplified by the fan. Other people have fans, but no one that I have seen spends their time circumnavigating the venue fanning everybody!

I often hear that I give the best hugs, as I am always available to make connections with people.

Hugging wasn't something that we did in our family, but now I always give my mother a big hug whenever I see her.

Most of my male friends from South London don't hug other men, but in Brighton, everybody loves a good hug!

Hugging for some men is something best left for the girls but I truly love to hug for at least 4 breaths, that way our bodies come together and you receive a jolt of love from my heart.

Speaking of hearts, I am known for wearing items of clothing with love hearts on them and have a dozen or so hearts in my flat.

It's all energy- and hearts convey the highest vibration of all.

Brighton is an amazing place to live, as there is such a great community spirit.

There are events going on all year round but, during the summer months it swells in size due to the tourists.

I have had the pleasure of massaging dozens of people at the beach and outside many of the landmarks and attractions. I never thought I'd end up busking for a living, but I have now earned money by massaging around town on many occasions and it has been challenging at times, but also a very rewarding experience.

In November 2011, I was invited to do massage for when Amma came to London for one of her three day specials.

It was the first time I had seen her, though many of my Zu friends knew her well.

She is the hugging , who has hugged over 30 million people around the world and has raised hundreds of millions of pounds for her charity.

At Alexander Palace in London thousands of people would queue merrily for hours to get their five second moment with this amazing woman.

I too had a hug from her which was beautiful, though not earth moving but she also gave me a sweet, rose petal and a bag of blessed ash.

Apparently, I was very fortunate to receive the ash, so immediately dabbed some on my forehead and continued massaging.

I arrived on the Tuesday afternoon and was there till Friday morning so, at night, slept in my car in the beautiful landscaped grounds.

The energy on the final evening reminded me of a festival.

There were so many friends that I had not seen in years there and I hugged them all.

There were also dozens of healers there, so the combined loving energy output was immense!

Collectively, we rose over £25,000 toward Amma's charity, that facilitates great work around the world. Amma is my role model now and she has maximized her healing gift to a level that impresses and inspires me!

Go Girl!

As I look back at my journey, I am proud to say that I have succeeded.

Nearly all of the items on my check list have been completed. I have become the world's first Massage SupaStar, created African Rhythms Massage, been featured in several magazines, at exhibitions and events, done motivational talks, worked in Harley Street and at The Hale Clinic, have successfully massaged at festivals and parties, been photographed by dozens of people while I work, painted by many artists, offered film roles, raised thousands for over a dozen charities, massaged over sixty people over eleven hours, inspired many to take up massage, received hundreds of testimonials from clients saying what an amazing treatment they had with me and have laid my hands on over ten thousand people to set them free from their mental, emotional, physical and spiritual pains.

But my final word on the search for recognition and fame is to be careful what you wish for, as although publicity equals more clients, it also raises your head above the parapet, exposing you to criticism and unwanted media attention. I now understand that this is why there are so very few well known healers, as most prefer a simple life far from the dazzling lights.

Social media has changed all that and now many healers have found the only way to connect with the world is to create a facebook account. Fortunately for me I am an open person so am completely comfortable communicating in this way.

CHAPTER 7
MY TRILEMA

"Had a lot of troubles in my life lately but today I feel the storm has passed." M x

What is a trilema, I hear you ask?

Well, let's just say it's a situation worse than a dilemma!

Although I have a happy heart and clear mindset, this has to be offset with the fact that I am continuously growing and thus make many mistakes.

Some of these mistakes can be painful to me and to others around me.

The most serious casualty of my journey, must be my marriage to Cathy.

Before my gift came to me, we were on a simple path of marriage, then to start a family, then to live happily ever after.

We did the first part and were moving onto the second at the time I received my calling.

Before then I was happy with the plan, but once I realised my purpose, my spirit had different plans. Also, because then I was a follower that agreed to things, sometimes out of being nice, I was not being authentic or true to myself, so there was an almighty battle inside of me on which direction to go.

I had my reasons why I felt this to be true, but didn't know how to communicate this in a peaceful and effective way.

I also realised that I was out of touch with my feelings, so would agree to things that I didn't like, so was very frustrated with myself.

Cathy was my first girlfriend I lived with so I was emotionally immature and found it very difficult to think for "us".

I was inconsiderate and ignorant at times, but thought that as long as I had good intentions that was ok.

I was type cast as a nice guy that smiled and was always courteous, but inside lurked a darker character that wanted to have a say too.

There were periods where I thought I was losing my mind and was not that nice husband that Cathy married, just a few years before.

Although I loved living in the country, I needed "me time" in London, doing the things I love most with my friends, but I just couldn't communicate my desires in a way that didn't end up hurting her.

Many say marriage is stressful, so I stuck with it hoping to find a solution, but in the end the best thing to do for both of us was to separate.

In the summer of 2008, I moved to Brighton to rebuild my shattered life.

Just weeks before, I was working at The Hale Clinic and had half a dozen journalists write stunning articles about me and I had plans to conquer the known Universe, but now I was depressed and needed the time and space to heal.

My mother suggested Brighton, as us Ijaws need water nearby to thrive, so every day I would go down to the beach and watch the waves roll in.

I thought I'd be back on my feet in a matter of weeks, but something more fundamental was occurring! Four years later, I now feel I am over my break up and life is shining brightly once more.

I cut off my dreadlocks at this time, as I wanted to start over and rebuild myself.

I'm not a Rastafarian, but simply liked hair that required little maintenance.

I preferred how I looked with dreadlocks, but it did make me look untidy, especially at this time of recession.

The shaven look was a surprise to many, but my mother was really happy because she grew up in a generation that looked down at anyone dumb enough to grow their hair in this way.

I also thought that I looked neater and more professional and that look made me more approachable to the business community from whom I was trying to attract work.

I was seeking answers and went to the Mind Body Spirit Festival at Brighton Racecourse.
I knew there would be mediums there who could see why things were not working for me.
As I walked in, I knew several of the therapists present and Claire Kirtland, the organiser of the event, asked me to massage, even though I didn't pre book a pitch.
Whilst walking around the hall I came across Andrew Kane, a huge, loving, golden souled medium who was doing a group reading.
I felt an instant connection with him and found out that he had a clinic in Brighton.
Andrew not only gave me great news about my future, but also let me use his clinic and recommended clients to me.

I stayed away from women for over a year, as I knew that my problems were within me and dating other women too soon would just complicate matters.
I found peace in music.
Brighton has a healthy reggae scene and it was here where no one knew me, the opportunity to start over.
I found the uplifting vibrations of roots reggae such a tonic for my sadness, that within a matter of weeks I was feeling better.
I have to thank my family and friends Andrew, Kate, Alex, and Lynn for supporting me physically and emotionally.
Since then many others have crossed my path to help heal me back to emotional wellness.

The true Magnus was someone far grander than the one married to Cathy.
The way I wanted to live was miles different to the shell of a man who was married.

Cathy was a good girl and wanted me to live like her, but I love colourful characters that have a foot either side of the law.
These are the people that I loved being around and these characters were the kind of people she prided herself in staying away from and having no part in her life.
Our marriage was doomed and it was me that made it that way.
My only regret was hurting a friend and her family, who gave me so much for five years.
Cathy, you opened my eyes to a better way of living and I thank you for that.
But part of owning my power was to learn to love and accept myself more, so I had to move on and follow my path.

In 2006 I sustained an eye injury that nearly blinded me in my right eye.
This was my better eye, so I found driving very difficult. I scratched my lens and no matter what I tried I couldn't see clearly.
For nearly two years, I struggled to see and to my surprise a week after moving to Brighton, perfect vision was restored.
Louise L. Hay says that eye problems relate to not wanting to acknowledge the future you're looking into, which gave me the belief that I'd made the correct decision to leave.

I learned many things about women, relationships, the countryside, and vegetarian food, business, marketing, branding, filing, being true to my word and not lying, from living with Cathy and because of her love, I am a better man.
The biggest lesson, however, has been the need to be authentic and the pain I can cause to my loved ones, when I am not.

Enough time has passed since having a woman in my life, so I was on the hunt for a companion.
I was jaded after five years with Cathy, so wasn't sure what kind of woman I was actually after.
Did I want a festival hippy chick with hairy armpits, or someone more refined?

There were many beautiful women around, but I realized how fussy I was, as looks alone wouldn't do.
I joined a couple of dating websites but never actually followed anyone up, as I prefer to meet people in the flesh.

Being a masseur made matters much more difficult, as although many woman would love my touch, most would not want a relationship with me, and to share my healing hands with others.
If you have any jealousy issues, then you seriously don't want to be my lady, as there were always women in my life and many of those are intelligent, spiritual and on point in their lives and were not afraid show their affection for me, as they feel comfortable in my space.
Though my massages can feel very loving, they are not sexual and though some people may think that I sleep around, I have a simple a strict rule.
If I massage you, then we cannot have sex, period.

One Tuesday evening in May 2009 I attended the Brighton Fringe Festival African Night Fever, situated in the Spiegel Tent on the Old Stein.
I arrived late after being at a Landmark seminar and was there to support the Nana Tsobi and Linos Wengara, the two headlining acts.
Both of them I knew previously, so knew it would be a great night of tribal sounds. The next Pure Natural Vibes was in five days' time so it was a no brainer to hand out flyers that evening.
I also had my trusty fan with me and danced around the room, fanning everyone and making friends.

There were many gorgeous women that night, but I got chatting to Elle at the end of the night.
Not only was she beautiful, but she also had a spiritual radiance that I had not come across before.
It was one of those instant connections, where the conversation flowed easily and the twinkles in our eyes were very noticeable.

We shared a sexual chemistry that made my heart flutter, so I knew I'd be seeing her again!

I saw her the following Friday, but we texted each other all week.

These were exciting days, as it had been years since I had enjoyed a good flirt.

The thought that I've met someone special lifted me, as I was excited about our next encounter.

We spent the following ten days together and chatted constantly. It was so different from being with Cathy.

I'd finally found someone who wasn't fazed by the company I kept, the music I loved and how I lived my life.

I just wanted more of this, as I had lost all hope of finding happiness again.

I met her family and have massaged nearly all of them. I love them all and am proud to have enjoyed several family occasions with them.

I particularly get on well with her 82 year old Gran, who is a real character.

Wales is a country that I have travelled to, but only the cities- so when I was invited to Fishguard for my birthday, I was blown away with how beautiful the scenery and people were.

Since then, I have spent many holidays in Wales with Elle's family.

Elle and my mother have a similar frequency and are both very powerful people that are not afraid to fight for what's fair.

Before meeting her, I knew very little about animals.

My mother in law had a dog called Tigger that I occasionally walked, but that was it! Elle really educated me in why people have animals around them.

Chuggy, her rag-doll cat made a connection within hours of me first coming over.

He is a lazy cat and will only come to you if your vibration is correct.

He would come over and lick my hand and display real affection.

I received a similar welcome from Alfie, her German shepherd. He was old and would usually attack strange men, but we got on just fine as I massaged his arthritic back legs.

I would get the same treatment from most of the pets of my clients, so began to trust my instincts and believe that animals played an important role in healing.

When we move to the country, we will get a rescue dog and possibly, some chickens, so I too can experience the healing love that comes from having animals around.

Meeting Elle has been the perfect antidote for me and she has helped heal me.

I love you, Elle. xxx

Brighton and Lewes, are deeply spiritual towns, so I have manifested the best community of friends I could have ever imagined, where I receive all the love necessary to fulfil my dreams and live my life in service.

During the writing of this book, I have been taken to some places that, had I known previously, I would not have started writing. People often come to me with depression and I instantly make them feel happier, clearer and send them on their merry way. But, for a few months, I was in the very same place, with no one to turn to for relief.

The demons that resided in my head took charge and a chain reaction of negativity filled my life.

I simply couldn't cope with my life and thought I'd lost it.

Many people think I'm crazy most of the time, but, for a period, I too believed that I'd lost the plot.

I spent weeks focussing on all the sadness going on in the world and thought what was the point in fighting on.

With the end of the known world coming at the end of 2012, the polar shift, solar flares, New World Order, HARRP, alien invasions, the collision of Planet X Niburu, false flag operations, engineered world recession, all the man made illnesses killing millions across the world and my financial situation spiralling out of control- I felt crushed by it all and couldn't find a way through.

Only when I stopped seeing myself as an individual and realised that this feeling was something shared by many of my friends, who are also healers, and others knowledgeable of what was going on a cosmic level, could I free myself from this destructive reality.

I also remembered that the Law of Attraction works whether I want it to or not, so spending all day thinking about death and destruction wasn't going to bring me peace and love.

By the summer of 2011, I had shed my heavy coat of depression and switched my mindset to positivity and prosperity and within a short time was full of vitality once more and back on the word processor.

Money problems have been a constant in my life and like many therapists I have found it really difficult to earn the necessary funds to pay all my bills. My spirit has kept me on my path touching people to earn a living though my mind has been persuaded to look at various multi level marketing opportunities that have distracted me with the promise of riches. They always say this will be the next big thing but if I give them my energy, when will I be the next big thing?

CHAPTER 8
THE FUTURE

"Since having massages with Magnus I have felt less stressed, clearer in thought, more energetic and happier with what I have. Originally, I came with a desire for muscular pain relief but have found myself re-attached to my spiritual side. Life seems a lot less confusing". B

Healing has taken me on a long and challenging journey that began many years ago.
The ball of healing energy that chose to frustrate me as a child has now blossomed and allowed me to find my purpose.
Life growing up was very painful at times and sometimes I wanted it to end, but my spirit was strong.
Acknowledging me as a healer was the start of an amazing adventure, of discovering how humans fall ill and our journey back to recovery.

This is my very first book, but no doubt there will be others, as I live a very colourful life and almost every day I touch someone or make a difference worth writing about.
There are nearly seven billion people on the planet and I cannot touch them all.
By writing books I can touch thousands or even millions of people.

I attended a T Harv Eker – Millionaire Mindset three-day seminar in London in the summer of 2011 and realised that if I were to reach a million people, then I would have to change some of the disempowering conversations I had about money.
I learned many things about myself over the three days, but probably the three most important things were that although I was a good giver, I was a terrible receiver and this would have to change if I wanted to attract wealth.

The next thing was that if I were to become rich, it would mean that I would have added value to the lives of many people. Finally, to believe that lucrative opportunities always come my way, something that immediately lit up my spirit to get into action and finish writing this book.

On the Monday after the weekend, I came home and found £836 in my flat.
Clearly there was an instant impact from this change of mindset, so I bought a car and invested the rest in my business.

Healing doesn't have to involve physical touch and many people do distance healing, working on sick people hundreds, or even thousands, of miles away.
We are all energy and our brain-waves can reach round the world to anyone we wish to heal.
The Internet and social media have made our world a very small place, so healing someone across the globe is no more difficult than healing someone across town.

Another way I share my healing with the world is by my uniquely blended massage balm that has been infused with my healing hands.
The balm is made from organic fair trade shea butter, mixed with essential oils and my healing energy.
So, no matter where you are in the world, you can experience my healing energy, directly onto your skin, in the comfort of your own home.
It's not just any massage balm, but one that can be used daily to enrich your skin and contains that special ingredient that penetrates far deeper than just your skin.

We live in an ever-changing world that appears to be getting more and more stressful by the day.
The veil is being lifted and our eyes are beginning to open to the state of the world and our environment.

We have realised that our governments have been lying to us, about pretty much every aspect of how the world really works. As a result, the public are now more open to alternative perspectives and points of view.

People are waking up to natural remedies and seeking the services of healers and holistic practitioners, as they realize that allopathic medicine is no longer the answer to all our illnesses and diseases.

We are becoming consciously aware of the planet and her needs and, if we continue to ignore what we know in our hearts to be true, we are doomed.

The world requires a new kind of leader, one that is not afraid to speak from their heart, inspire others to follow their hearts and stand up and be counted.

The world requires leaders that are respected for their actions and not merely their fancy words.

I consider myself one of those leaders, a Warrior of the Light.

My healing hands do not discriminate, but work on all people, whether good or bad, black or white and of all ages.

Within seconds, the recipient feels a connection with their soul and they feel an instant transmission with Source energy.

Words alone cannot describe this feeling.

Suddenly their focus has shifted from their day-to-day stresses to a worldly peace.

They feel grounded and back to a familiar place, as if they have been transported back to their mother's womb.

I am proud to touch people and proud that I give people around me the freedom to be touched.

Some factions of the media may print unkind reports about the dangers of complementary medicines but I stand shoulder to shoulder with my fellow healers, whose only wish is to help others in a natural way.

Many people use the excuse that they don't have the money to help others.

I disagree with that because I know that once you have the intention to help, opportunities to help reveal themselves all around you.

Sure, if you had more money there are things you can pay for that need to be bought, but there is a lot to be said for simply listening to someone and physically comforting them with your love.

There are many healers out there that don't know that they are healers because they don't fit the stereotype, but inside they know that what they are doing is not their purpose.

They are stuck doing jobs that rob the best years of their lives, when instead they could be making a difference by healing.

Some work in offices that are full of stressed and sick people that would benefit hugely from a hug, a massage or simply the gentle stroke on their back.

But legislation in the workplace outlaws this as sexual harassment, so, out of fear, people avoid bodily contact.

I have been invited into offices just like this, with hundreds of desks on a single floor.

Everybody that I touched lit up and really appreciated being massaged while they sat at their desks.

Many were frustrated with their jobs, but were too afraid to make the change to something fulfilling.

There are others who know that they are healers, but fear the disapproval of colleagues, friends and family or the lack of kudos or respectability.

But society is changing and people are beginning to respect the difference an energy healer can make, especially as so many scientific studies are proving that what we do is not make believe.

My plan is to continue healing and shining my light by any means necessary.

Whether by touch, talking, texting, teaching, dancing, fanning, radio and TV interviews, books, cd's, videos and using the internet.

Currently, most of my healing has taken place in the UK but I would like to spread my wings and fly around the world doing healing wherever my services are required.

I have enjoyed an amazing journey so far, but have many years ahead of me, so would like to heal as many people as possible.

If you're reading this from somewhere far from the UK and want me to come to your country to heal, then please get in touch and let's make it happen.

Thank you for reading my book and I hope it continues to be a source of healing for you.

I completed the PDF version of my book in March 2012 and in the last paragraph I say I want to to the country, have amazing gatherings and start a family with Elle.

Well, many of the things that I wished for have come to pass, but you can hear about it all, at length, in my next book.

I have been saying for a year now that I didn't want the paperback to be printed until I had left my flat in Brighton and moved to the country, because it didn't feel right on an energetic level. Calling myself a Massage SupaStar and living in a one bed flat, where I massaged in my lounge just wasn't congruent. The Universe clearly agreed, because within three months of completing that version, I had moved to Plantation Healing Retreat.

We had been looking at rural properties in the midst of nature for some time, but the one we had our hearts set on, was taken off the market and we were gutted! So, to find ourselves living in our dream location, out in the middle of the English countryside, was a miracle! I am eternally grateful to the Universe for making our dreams a reality.

Since moving to Plantation Healing Retreat, life has got much more interesting! Many more people believe in what I have to say and what I am up for in life. I have received many opportunities to come and shine my light at retreats, festivals, parties, charity fundraisers and other cultural and healing events. It has been amazing! Marketing Plantation Healing Retreat has been a joy, as I know that once you commit to coming, you have committed to your recovery; as many visitors will testify. Telling people about this wonderful place is much easier than selling Magnus the Masseur, as it sells itself!

My health has improved; not surprising after being bathed 24/7 in nature's energy. The combination of Universal energy flowing through the land and through my hands, has healed many since moving here and each treatment has felt so special. We have had a number of gatherings and retreats here and all who have attended have left feeling that their stresses have been reduced. I've always wished to have a fire-pit in my garden, where friends can gather to share thoughts about life and watch the stars. Now we have one, we have sat through the night to watch the Solstice sun rise, enjoyed acoustic sessions and simply meditated to the dancing flames.

I have never owned a pet before and was actually afraid of dogs after being chased by one as a child. Elle used to have four dogs , but hadn't had one for the past 5 years whilst living in the city, so was eager to get a dog once we moved to the country. We went along to the R.S.P.C.A. to look at the rescue dogs and we saw this gangly lurcher cross, Rhodesian Ridgeback puppy, named Kane, leaping up at the bars, trying to get our attention. He was one of those dogs that would have no trouble being re-homed, so we knew we had to act fast, if we wanted him. Within a week of first setting eyes on him, he was living with us at Plantation Healing Retreat!

Learning how to manage a dog was a real shock to the system and to have to consider the needs of a puppy was something I had no experience of, but had to master. I watched several episodes of Caesar Milan-The Dog Whisperer, to learn how to be Kane's alpha and pack leader. Kane kind of reminds me of myself, as he doesn't understand how big and strong he is and the power he wields. He would only be playing, but sometimes would leap up onto his hind legs in excitement and frighten people who were inexperienced with dogs. But, to my surprise, I have bonded really well with Kane and together we have explored some of the most scenic walks in the area. If it were not for Kane, I would have not have gone on many of the beautiful walks that I have and seen so much nature. He has enriched my life, in ways I never thought possible.

In August, I was nominated for the Conscious World Awards; Inspirational Body worker/Holistic Practitioner Award. I have never been nominated for such an award, but felt exalted and uplifted to learn that many people had been paying attention to my efforts and wanted to recognize me formally. Of course I would like to win, but it has already given me a boost, knowing that I am one of the best at what I do and someone deserving of such an award.

Where next?

Book signing across the world, speaking engagements, TV, radio, newspaper and magazines articles workshops, retreats and laying my hands on thousands more people at parties, events. I plan to be financially free, so I can perform African Rhythms Massages at Plantation Healing Retreat, across the country and around the world. Help my brothers and sisters in Bayelsa State and fulfil my fathers dream.

Thank you reading my story and I hope it has inspired you to Shine Your Light and Touch the World.

One Massage,
Many Possibilities.

Magnus Woyingi-Kuro Agugu
www.magnusthemasseur.co.uk